OXFORD*modern*Playscripts

Johnny
and the
Dead

Terry Pratchett

adapted by
Stephen Briggs

D1340424

OXFORD
UNIVERSITY PRESS

Great Clarendon Street, Oxford OX2 6DP

Oxford University Press is a department of the University of Oxford.
It furthers the University's objective of excellence in research, scholarship, and
education by publishing worldwide in

Oxford New York
Auckland Cape Town Dar es Salaam Hong Kong Karachi Kuala Lumpur
Madrid Melbourne Mexico City Nairobi New Delhi Taipei Toronto Shanghai

With offices in
Argentina Austria Brazil Chile Czech Republic France Greece Guatemala
Hungary Italy Japan South Korea Poland Portugal Singapore Switzerland
Thailand Turkey Ukraine Vietnam

Oxford is a registered trade mark of Oxford University Press
in the UK and in certain other countries
This adaptation of **Johnny and the Dead** © Stephen Briggs 1996
Activity section © Jenny Roberts 2003

The moral rights of the authors have been asserted

Database right Oxford University Press (maker)

This edition first published 2003

British Library Cataloguing in Publication Data

Data available

ISBN 0 19 831492 2

10 9 8 7 6 5 4

Printed in and bound by Creative Print and Design Wales, Ebbw Vale

Acknowledgements

Extract from *Johnny and the Dead* by Terry Pratchett, published by Corgi,
copyright © Terry Pratchett 1995, reprinted by permission of Transworld
Publishers, a division of The Random House Group Ltd.

The Publisher would like to thank Hulton Getty for permission to reproduce
photographs on page 93.

Illustrations are by Neil Chapman.

Contents

General Introduction

With a fresh, modern look, this classroom-friendly series boasts an exciting range of authors – from Pratchett to Chaucer – whose works have been expertly adapted by such well-known and popular writers as Philip Pullman and David Calcutt. We have also divided the titles available (see page 96) into subcategories – Oxford *Classic Playscripts* and Oxford *Modern Playscripts* – to make it even easier for you to think about titles, and periods, you wish to study.

Many teachers use Oxford *Playscripts* to study the format, style, and structure of playscripts with their students; for speaking and listening assignments; to initiate discussion of relevant issues in class; to meet the Drama objectives of the Framework; as an introduction to the novel of the same title; and to introduce the less able or willing to pre-1914 literature.

At the back of each Oxford *Playscript*, you will find a brand new Activity section, which not only addresses the points above, but also features close text analysis, and activities that provide support for underachieving readers and act as a springboard for personal writing. Furthermore, the new Activity sections now match precisely the Framework Objectives for Teaching English at Key Stage 3; a chart mapping the Objectives - and the activities that cover them – can be found at the beginning of each section. Many schools will simply read through the play in class with no staging at all, and the Activity sections have been written with this in mind, with individual activities ranging from debates and designing campaign posters to writing extra scenes or converting parts of the original novels into playscript form.

For those of you, however, who do wish to take to the stage, we have included, where necessary, 'A Note on Staging' – a section dedicated to suggesting ways of staging the play, as well as examining the props and sets you may wish to use.

Above all, we hope you will enjoy using Oxford *Playscripts*, be it on the stage or in the classroom.

What the Author Says

It's not a good idea to ask a tightrope walker how they keep their balance, and it's not a good idea to ask an author why they wrote something in a certain way. But here goes …

I wrote a lot of *Johnny and the Dead* because I was angry. The little town I grew up in was something like Blackbury, and it has changed in the same way. Little shops have been killed off by a big supermarket. There are now about a million building society offices in the high street and hardly anywhere to buy food. It used to have its own council, even its own coat of arms. Now it's run from some other town ten miles away. It's not a place where people live anymore, it's just a place they park their cars.

Other things pointed the way towards the book. I actually met a man called Tommy Atkins, who *had* fought all the way through the First World War and was immensely proud of his name. And I was puzzled by the way in which the dead, in our society, always seem to be represented as evil. After all, they were our *ancestors*. Other societies don't think in the same way – some would gently dry grandad out when he passed away and then prop him high on the mountain somewhere to watch over his descendants (don't try this at home).

I wanted to write a book that said: the past might not have been better, but it is important and it was real. Real people lived and died. They weren't just jerky figures in old newsreels. Everything around us is the result of things they did, good *and* bad. We might learn something if we try to work out the difference. Some people feel that a concern for the past is 'against progress', but progress just means travel and is not automatically in a good direction – sometimes it makes the world a better place, and other times it means bad things happen fast.

I brought the Pals in because most of the Dead that Johnny meets are, well, funny, and I wanted to balance this up a little. I wanted him to understand that white-haired old Tommy Atkins was *also* a young man on a terrible battlefield. Tommy Atkins was not a lot older than Johnny when the Pals went off to war (some boys even lied about their age to get into the army) and I wanted

Johnny and his friends to realize that if they'd been born earlier, it might have been *them*. And I wanted to say that the past is all around us, and sometimes we owe it something.

But if I was honest, I'd say that I also brought the Pals in because the image of the young ghosts of his friends marching back to greet Thomas Atkins when he died was *right*. I wasn't sure why, but I knew it was. Sometimes things just happen that way. Some things you don't work out in your head.

Terry Pratchett

What the Adaptor Says

I first encountered Terry Pratchett and his writings when I wrote to him to ask if I could adapt one of his books, *Wyrd Sisters*, for the amateur stage. That was in 1990 and since then we have gone on to work together on various projects, mostly connected with his Discworld series of novels.

Like much of Terry Pratchett's writing, *Johnny and the Dead* appears on the surface to be a fantasy story, but closer examination shows that it is firmly rooted in reality. In *Johnny and the Dead* it is easy to see that the living's attitude to the dead neatly reflects the young and healthy's attitude to the elderly or disabled. Indeed, we can also see how adults react to children and the way that those at either end of the scale (the very young and the very old – or the dead) often get along better than the generations in between.

The methods used to adapt a novel for the stage are as varied as the authors you try to adapt. Some authors make heavy use of narrative and the adaptor has then to weave that into the play as well, if they are to keep to the spirit of the original work. Some authors, such as Charles Dickens and Terry Pratchett, write very good dialogue, which helps the action to leap from the page. This makes the adaptor's job easier – whole chunks of text can be lifted straight from the book into the play.

It is difficult to be hard and fast about 'rules' for adapting books, but here are a few useful guidelines that I do try to stick to.

- Do not change the principal plot. There is no point in calling a play *Bram Stoker's Dracula* if you are then going to have Dracula surviving at the end and starting up a flourishing law firm in Whitby.
- Never sacrifice 'real' scenes in order to add in some of your own. After all, you have chosen to adapt the author's work because, presumably, you admire their writing. If you think you can improve on their humour/drama/characterization you should really be writing your own plots and not torturing theirs.
- Use the author's dialogue whenever possible. Same as above, really. Also try to have the same character saying the same lines as they do in the book – rather than giving them to another character.
- Don't add characters. Stick to those the author has given you.
- Don't be afraid to cut material. After all, you are trying to squeeze a three-hundred-page novel into a two-hour play; you just can't fit everything in, so don't try. Anything which does not help the main plot move forward should be on your list for potential dumping if the play overruns.

Because this play is as likely to be used for reading in a classroom as for a stage production, I've also tried to keep the amount of stage directions to a minimum. Reading lots of instructions is *very* boring. However, if the characters just stand there and talk at each other in a performance of the script, the audience will find this very boring, too. The trick is to find things for the characters to do that make the things they say more effective.

I have tried to ensure that the special effects I have mentioned should be either easily achievable or not essential. I have also tried to arrange it so that the play can be performed with the minimum amount of scenery; in Terry's books the plot and the characters are the important things. Any scenic or other effects you can afford to conjure up on top of that are a bonus.

Stephen Briggs

A Note on Staging

Costumes and Props

Generally, you will need to consider when the Dead died (as they are mostly likely to be dressed in clothes from that period), and how old they were.

Props you may need include:

Johnny: a schoolbag; a ghetto blaster; a pink sheet; a pocket TV.

Wobbler: a schoolbag; a Dracula costume.

Bigmac: a 'sharpened stake and a hammer'; a newspaper; a skeleton costume; a 'length of lead piping'.

Yo-less: a CD; a Baron Samedi costume, including a bowler hat.

Nurse: a cardboard box containing a pipe, a tobacco tin, a 'huge penknife', a scrapbook, a box with medals, and a photograph.

The Play at a Glance

The outline of the play below highlights the props or scenery you may want to consider for a performance.

Scene One *The cemetery*

This set will need to include gravestones and greenery; Alderman Bowler's tomb with 'an impressive door, over which is carved 'Pro Bono Publico'; William Stickers' headstone – 'William Stickers. 1897 – 1949. Workers of the World Unit'; Eric Grimm's headstone – 'Eric Grimm 1885 – 1927'; Vicenti's grave – 'Dead impressive' with 'a big arch'; lots of tombstones featuring crosses (in Scene Three, Yo-less says 'there's crosses all over the place').

Scene Two *A school classroom*

A newspaper. You may wish to include: desks, chairs, a whiteboard, a bin.

Scene Three *The cemetery*

As above.

Scene Four *Grandad's house*

An armchair; a local paper; a stool; (optional) a 'little transistor radio'.

Scene Five *The library*

Shelves of books; tables and chairs; 'old papers'.

Scene Six *The cemetery*

As above, plus the 'little transistor radio'.

Scene Seven *The shopping mall*

A bench. You may also wish to include: bins, plants, shoppers.

Scene Eight *An old people's home*

Armchairs. You may also wish to include: plants.

Scene Nine *A phone box*

Note: This is situated just outside the cemetery fence. The set will need to incorporate both sides of the fence, as Eric Grimm remains within the cemetery boundary throughout.

Scene Ten *The cemetery chapel, then outside the chapel*

Pews (inside); a bench (outside).

Note: For this scene, the set needs to take into account both the interior of the chapel and area outside the chapel.

Scene Eleven *The canal bank*

Litter, including a 'battered old TV set'.

Note: This is situated just outside the cemetery fence. The set will need to incorporate both sides of the fence, as Eric Grimm remains within the cemetery boundary throughout.

Scene Twelve *The Civic Centre*

'Rows of chairs in front of a table on a raised platform'; sheets of paper (handouts).

Scene Thirteen *A street in Blackbury*

Shop fronts, including Boots, Mothercare, and 'Spud-u-like'. You may also wish to include: lamp posts, litter bins, street signs.

Scene Fourteen *The Cemetery*

As above.

Scene Fifteen *The Cemetery*

As above.

Characters

In order of their appearance on stage:

Johnny Maxwell — a twelve-year-old boy who discovers he can talk to the Dead in the local cemetery

Wobbler Johnson — Johnny's school friend

Alderman Thomas Bowler — one of the Dead; a member of Blackbury Council when alive; he wears civic robes

Grandad — Johnny's grandad

William Stickers — one of the Dead; a communist when alive; he has a huge black beard and wears gold-rimmed spectacles

Yo-less — Johnny's school friend

Bigmac — Johnny's school friend

Antonio Vicenti — one of the Dead; ran a joke shop and worked as an escapologist and children's entertainer when alive; wears a red carnation in his button hole

Mrs Sylvia Liberty — one of the Dead; a suffragette who campaigned for votes for women when alive

Solomon Einstein — one of the Dead; a famous taxidermist when alive; a keen thinker

Addison Vincent Fletcher — one of the Dead; invented a form of telephone when alive

Stanley 'Wrong Way' Roundaway — one of the Dead (non-speaking); played for Blackbury Wanderers when alive; famous for scoring own goals; wears a 1930s football kit

Eric Grimm — one of the Dead; disapproves of the behaviour of the other Dead; has a mysterious past

Radio Announcer — (voice only) on BBC Radio Blackbury

DJ	(voice only) on BBC Radio Blackbury
Johnny's Mum	(non-speaking)
Johnny's Gran	(non-speaking)
Nurse	works at Sunshine Acres Old People's Home
Mad Jim	(voice only) DJ for BBC Radio Blackbury; hosts 'Mad Jim's Late-Night Explosion'
Mr Ronald Atterbury	from the British Legion
Private Tommy Atkins	a young soldier from the First World War (non-speaking)
Ms Ethel Liberty	a representative of Blackbury Council
Mr Bowler	a representative of United Amalgamated Consolidated Holdings
Woman in the Audience	at the meeting at the civic centre
Radio Interviewer	(voice only) for BBC Radio Blackbury
First Man] **Second Man**]	thugs hired to wreck the cemetery
Police Officer	(non-speaking)
Police Officer	who arrests the second man
Other Non-speaking Roles	other dead people (if required); old people at Sunshine Acres; soldiers from the First World War; people at the meeting at the civic centre

SCENE 1

*The cemetery. **Johnny** walks onto the stage, carrying his schoolbag.*
He sits on a tombstone and addresses the audience.

Johnny	I really discovered the cemetery after I started living at Grandad's, after my parents split up. I started taking a short-cut through here instead of going home on the bus. My pal Wobbler thinks it's spooky …

Wobbler enters, carrying a schoolbag.

Wobbler	Why do we have to go home this way? I think it's spooky.
Johnny	*[Still talking to the audience]* But I think it's quite … friendly. Peaceful. Once you forget about all the skeletons underground, of course.

*Wobbler sits next to **Johnny**.*

Wobbler	It's Hallowe'en next week. I'm having a party; you have to come as something horrible. So don't bother to find a disguise.
Johnny	Thanks.
Wobbler	You notice how there's a lot more Hallowe'en stuff in the shops these days?
Johnny	It's because of Bonfire Night. Too many people were blowing themselves up with fireworks, so they invented Hallowe'en, where you just wear masks and stuff.

Wobbler	My mum's friend, Mrs Nugent, says all that sort of thing is tampering with the occult.
Johnny	Probably is.
Wobbler	She says witches are abroad on Hallowe'en.
Johnny	What …? Like … Majorca, and places?
Wobbler	*[Not very certain on this point]* 'Spose so.
Johnny	Makes sense, I suppose. They probably get out-of-season bargains, being old ladies. My aunt can go anywhere on the buses for almost nothing and she's not even a witch.
Wobbler	Don't see what Mrs Nugent is worried about then. It ought to be a lot safer round here, with all the witches on holiday.
Johnny	I saw a thing in a book once, about these people in Mexico or somewhere, where they all go down to the cemetery for a big fiesta at Hallowe'en every year. Like, they don't see why people should be left out of things just because they're dead.
Wobbler	Yuk. A picnic? In the actual cemetery? You'd get glowing green hands pushing up through the earth and nicking the sarnies.
Johnny	Don't think so. Anyway … they don't eat sarnies in Mexico. They eat tort … um, tort … something.
Wobbler	*[Confidently]* Tortoises.
Johnny	Yeah?

*A new thought occurs to **Wobbler**.*

Wobbler	I bet. I bet … I bet you wouldn't dare knock on one of those doors. You know, one of them doors on those big gravestones. I bet something really horrible would come lurchin' out!

***Wobbler** stands and lurches about a bit, arms stretched out in front of him. Then another new thought occurs to him.*

Wobbler	'Ere, my dad says all this is going to be built on. He says the council sold it to some big company for five pence, cos it was costing too much to keep it going. It's going to be offices and things.

Johnny	I'd have given them a pound just to leave it as it is. I bet the people here wouldn't be very happy about it. If they knew.

Johnny points at Alderman Bowler's tomb, which has an impressive door, over which is carved 'Pro Bono Publico'.

Johnny	I bet he'd be really angry.

He crosses to the door and knocks.

Wobbler	*[Looking worried]* Hey! You mustn't do that!

Johnny knocks again. The door opens and Alderman Thomas Bowler steps out. Although his face is a bit on the pale side, he looks comparatively normal, and is dressed in his civic robes.

Alderman Bowler	Yes?

Johnny cries out in surprise and takes a couple of steps back, bumping into Wobbler.

Wobbler	*[Startled]* What?
Johnny	The door's opened! Can't you see it?
Wobbler	No! No I can't! There's no point in your trying to frighten me, you know. Er … look, anyway, I'm late. Um. Bye!

Wobbler starts to walk off, but quickly breaks into a run. Johnny walks over to Alderman Bowler.

Alderman Bowler	What is it you want?
Johnny	Are you dead?

Alderman Bowler points to the sign over his doorway.

Alderman Bowler	See what it says there?
Johnny	Er …
Alderman Bowler	It says nineteen hundred and six. It was a very good funeral, I gather. I didn't attend myself … er … rather, I did, but not so's I could actually observe events, if you get my meaning. What was it you were wanting?

Johnny	*[Not quite sure what he does want]* Er … what … er … what does 'Pro Bono Publico' mean?
Alderman Bowler	It means 'for the public good'.
Johnny	Oh. Well, thank you. Thanks very much.
Alderman Bowler	Was that all?
Johnny	Yes.
Alderman Bowler	I didn't think it could be anything important. I haven't had a visitor since nineteen twenty-three. And even then they'd got the name wrong. And – they were Americans! Oh well, goodbye then.
	*Alderman Bowler freezes. **Johnny** takes a few steps away from him and speaks directly to the audience.*
Johnny	I was about to go home, and I thought 'if I go I'll never know what happens next'.
	*He turns and walks back to **Alderman Bowler**.*
Johnny	You're dead, right?
Alderman Bowler	Oh yes. It's one of those things one is pretty certain about.
Johnny	Are you a ghost?
Alderman Bowler	Good heavens, no! I'm just dead.
Johnny	You're no good at dancing, are you?
Alderman Bowler	I used to be able to waltz quite well.
Johnny	No, I meant … sort of … like this *[doing a passable impression of Michael Jackson moonwalking]* you know, with your feet.
Alderman Bowler	That looks very energetic.
Johnny	And you have to go 'Ow!'.
Alderman Bowler	I should think anyone would, dancing like that.
Johnny	No, no, I mean … no, never mind. But look, I don't see how you can be dead and walking and talking at the same time.

Alderman Bowler	That's probably because of relativity. *[Moonwalking stiffly across the path]* Like this, was it? Ouch!
Johnny	Yeah, a bit. How do you mean … relativity?
Alderman Bowler	I'm not too sure. Einstein explains it better.
Johnny	What, *Albert* Einstein?
Alderman Bowler	*[Still doing a rather inexpert moonwalk]* Who?
Johnny	He was a famous scientist.
Alderman Bowler	No, I meant Solomon Einstein. He was a famous taxidermist in Cable Street. Very keen thinker. Got knocked down by a car in nineteen thirty-two.

It has been getting darker.

| Johnny | I think I'd better be getting home. It's getting late, anyway. |
| Alderman Bowler | *[Still moonwalking]* I think I'm getting the hang of this. Call any time you like. I'm always in. That's something you learn to be good at, when you're dead. Er, 'Ow!' was it? |

Alderman Bowler moonwalks off stage as Johnny comes downstage to address the audience.

| Johnny | And that was the first time I'd seen one of the Dead from the cemetery. It wasn't the last, though. The next day, I was walking through the cemetery with my grandad. |

Grandad enters.

Johnny	That was when I met William Stickers.
Grandad	It's disgusting, what the council are doing. Selling off this cemetery, and for what? Another flippin' office block! There's history in here.
Johnny	Alderman Thomas Bowler.
Grandad	Never heard of 'im. I was referring to him. *[Pointing to a headstone]* William Stickers.
Johnny	Was he famous?

Grandad	Nearly famous. Nearly famous. You've heard of Karl Marx?
Johnny	He invented communism, didn't he?
Grandad	Right. Well, William Stickers didn't. But he'd have been Karl Marx if Karl Marx hadn't beaten him to it.

Grandad looks at the headstone, which is visible to the audience. It reads: 'William Stickers. 1897–1949. Workers of the world unit'.

Grandad	A great man.
Johnny	*[Reading the writing on the headstone]* Workers of the world unit? What was the 'world unit'?
	***William Stickers** enters. **Johnny** sees him but does not react yet.*
Grandad	It should have been 'unite'. 'Workers of the world unite.' They ran out of money before they did the 'e'. It was a scandal. He was a hero of the working class. He would have fought in the Spanish Civil War except he got on the wrong boat.
Johnny	What was he like? Was he a big man with a huge black beard and gold-rimmed spectacles?
Grandad	That's right. Seen pictures, have you?
Johnny	No. Not exactly.
Grandad	I'm going down the shops. Want to come?
Johnny	No, thanks. Er … I'm going round to Wobbler's.
Grandad	OK. See you.

Grandad exits.

Johnny	*[To **William Stickers**]* Hello.
William Stickers	It *was* a scandal, them not giving me the 'e'. You'd think somebody would have stumped up the extra couple of bob. What's your name, comrade?
Johnny	Johnny Maxwell.
William Stickers	What year is this, Johnny Maxwell?
Johnny	Nineteen ninety-five.
William Stickers	Ah! And have the downtrodden masses risen up to overthrow the capitalist oppressors in the glorious name of communism?
Johnny	Um? You mean like Russia and stuff? When they shot the Tsar?
William Stickers	Oh, I know *that*. I mean, what's been happening since nineteen forty-nine? No one tells us anything in here.
Johnny	Er, well … tell you what … can you read a newspaper if I bring one in?
William Stickers	Of course, but it's hard to turn the pages.
Johnny	Um. Are there a lot of you in here?
William Stickers	Hah! Most of them don't bother. They just aren't prepared to make the effort.
Johnny	Can you … you know … walk around? Cos you could get into things for free and so on.
William Stickers	It's hard to go far. It's not really allowed.
Johnny	Oh yes. I read in a book once that ghosts can't move around much.
William Stickers	Ghost!? Ghost!? I'm not a ghost! *[Starting to exit]* And don't you forget that paper, comrade!

***William Stickers** exits. Blackout.*

SCENE 2

*A school classroom. **Yo-less**, **Wobbler**, and **Bigmac** enter and sit at some desks. **Johnny** enters and joins them.*

Yo-less	Hello, Johnny. We were just talking about you. You been in that cemetery again?
Johnny	*[Defensively]* Yes.
Wobbler	Why do you go there? It's a dump. Well, the canal bank behind it is, anyway: old prams, burst settees, busted TVs …
Bigmac	Yeah, and on the other side is that waste ground that used to be the boot factory.
Yo-less	They're going to build an office building on that site. It was in the papers. *[Pulling out a copy of the local paper]* Look.
Johnny	*[Taking the paper]* It's huge. That'll take up more land than that factory site! *[Reading]* An Exciting Development for United Amalgamated Consolidated Holdings: Forward to the Future!
Wobbler	What do United Amalgamated Consolidated Holdings actually do?
Johnny	It says here they're a multi-national information-retrieval and enhancement facility. It says they'll provide three hundred new jobs.
Yo-less	For all the people who used to work at the Blackbury rubber boot factory. It all seems a bit pointless.
Wobbler	Hey! How are your ghosts getting on?
Johnny	No, not ghosts. They don't like being called ghosts. They're just … dead. I suppose it's like not calling people handicapped or backward.
Yo-less	Politically incorrect.
Wobbler	You mean they want to be called … post-senior citizens.
Yo-less	Breathily challenged.

Bigmac	Vertically disadvantaged.
Yo-less	What? You mean they're short?
Bigmac	Buried.
Wobbler	How about zombies?

*Wobbler staggers around, doing a 'zombie' walk, and grabs **Yo-less** by the throat.*

Yo-less	*[Pushing him away]* No, you've got to have a body to be a zombie. You're not really dead, you just get fed this secret voodoo mixture of fish and roots.
Wobbler	Fish n' roots? I bet it's a real adventure going down the chippie in voodoo country.
Bigmac	*[To Yo-less]* You ought to know about voodoo.
Yo-less	Why?
Bigmac	Well, cos you're West Indian, right?
Yo-less	What? You know all about druids, do you?
Bigmac	No.
Yo-less	Well, there you are then.
Johnny	No, look, you're not taking it seriously. I really saw them!
Wobbler	Yeah, but you once said you'd seen the Loch Ness monster in your goldfish pond.
Johnny	All right, but …
Bigmac	And then there was the lost city of the Incas.
Johnny	Well, I found it, didn't I?
Yo-less	Yes, but it wasn't that lost, was it? Behind Tesco's isn't exactly lost.
Johnny	Yes. Yes. All right. But, you'll come down after school, won't you?

Wobbler	Well …
Johnny	Not scared are you? You ran away before. When the Alderman came out.
Wobbler	I never saw no Alderman. Anyway, I just ran away to wind you up.
Johnny	You certainly had me fooled. All right then. All three of you. After school.
Bigmac	After 'Cobbers'.
Johnny	This is more important than some Aussie soap opera.
Bigmac	Yes, but tonight Janine is going to tell Mick that Doraleen took Ron's surfboard …
Johnny	All right then. After 'Cobbers'.
Yo-less	I've got some geography homework.
Johnny	We haven't got any.
Yo-less	No, but I thought if I did an extra essay on rainforests I could pull up my marks average.
Johnny	You're weird. All right. Let's meet up later. Six o'clock. At Bigmac's place, cos that's near the cemetery. Weird, really.
Yo-less	What is?
Johnny	Well, there's a huge cemetery for dead people and all the living people are crammed up in that multi-storey block of flats where Bigmac lives. I mean, it sounds like someone got something wrong …
Bigmac	Six o'clock, then.
Wobbler	But it'll be getting dark by then.
Johnny	Not scared, are you?
Wobbler	Me? Scared? Huh! Me? Scared? Me? Scared?

Blackout.

SCENE 3

Johnny, Wobbler, Bigmac, and Yo-less are now in the cemetery. Bigmac is hiding something behind his back. It is getting dark. Throughout the scene, Johnny is the only one of the living who can see The Dead. Wobbler, Bigmac, and Yo-less must react as though Johnny is the only other person onstage.

Wobbler	*[Looking nervously around him]* Scared? Me?

Yo-less puts a hand on Wobbler's shoulder. Wobbler yells.

Wobbler	Aaah!
Yo-less	Hey, don't panic. Look, there's crosses all over the place. See, it's sort of like a church, really.
Wobbler	Yes, but I'm an atheist.
Yo-less	Then you shouldn't believe in ghosts …
Bigmac	Post-senior citizens.
Johnny	Bigmac?
Bigmac	Yeah?
Johnny	What are you holding behind your back?

Bigmac produces a sharpened stake and a hammer.

Johnny	Bigmac!
Bigmac	Well, you never know …
Johnny	Leave them here!

Bigmac	Oh, all right.

Bigmac puts down the hammer and the stake.

Yo-less	Anyway, it's not stakes for ghosts. That's for vampires.
Wobbler	*[Not much reassured by this]* Oh, thank you!
Johnny	Look, this is just the cemetery. It's not Transylvania! There's just dead people here! Dead people are just people who were living once! A few years ago they were just mowing lawns and putting up Christmas decorations and being people's grandparents. They're nothing to be frightened of!
Yo-less	Yes … It's peaceful, isn't it?
Bigmac	Quiet as the grave. *[He laughs]*
Johnny	A lot of people come for walks here. I mean, the park's miles away, and all it's got is grass. This place has got bushes and plants and trees, and …
Yo-less	Environment. And probably some ecology as well.

Wobbler crosses to Antonio Vicenti's grave.

Wobbler	Hey, look at this grave. Dead impressive. But why has it got such a big arch on it?
Yo-less	That's just showing off. There's probably a sticker on the back saying, 'My Other Grave is a Porch'.
Johnny	*[He thinks this is a bit irreverent]* Yo-less!

Antonio Vicenti enters.

Antonio Vicenti	Actually, I think that was very funny. He is a very funny boy.
Johnny	Oh. Hello.

Wobbler, Bigmac, and Yo-less watch Johnny talking 'to himself' in amazement.

Antonio Vicenti	And what was the joke exactly?
Johnny	Well, you can get these stickers for cars, you see, and they say 'My Other Car is a Porsche'. It's a sort of sports car.

Antonio Vicenti	*[Laughing]* Oh yes. Back in the old country I used to do entertainment for kiddies. On Saturdays. At parties. The Great Vicenti and Ethel. I like to laugh.
Johnny	The old country?
Antonio Vicenti	The alive country.
Wobbler	You don't fool us. There's no one there.
Antonio Vicenti	And I did escapology, too.
Yo-less	You're just talking to the air.
Johnny	Escapology?
Antonio Vicenti	Escaping from things. Sacks and chains and handcuffs and so on. Like the Great Houdini? My greatest trick involved getting out of a locked sack underwater while wearing twenty feet of chain and three pairs of handcuffs.
Johnny	Gosh. How often did you do that?
Antonio Vicenti	Nearly once.
Wobbler	Come on, joke over.
Johnny	Shut up, this is interesting.
Antonio Vicenti	And you're John Maxwell. The Alderman told us about you.
Johnny	Us?
	*Antonio Vicenti nods in the direction over Johnny's shoulder. Johnny turns and sees **The Dead** – **Alderman Bowler, Mrs Sylvia Liberty, Solomon Einstein, William Stickers, Addison Vincent Fletcher**, and **Stanley 'Wrong Way' Roundaway** – moving on to the stage. They are surrounded by mist (created by dry ice or smoke pellets).*
Yo-less	He's not joking. Look at his face.
Wobbler	Johnny? Are you all right?
Bigmac	It's gone cold.

Wobbler	*[His voice shaking]* We ought to be getting back. I ought to be doing my homework.
Bigmac	Blimey! You *must* be frightened!
Wobbler	Shut up!
Johnny	*[To his friends]* You can't see them, can you? They're all around you but you can't see them!
Antonio Vicenti	The living generally can't see the dead. It's for their own good, I expect.
Bigmac	Come on. Stop mucking about.
Yo-less	Hang on. There's something odd …
Alderman Bowler	John Maxwell! We must talk to you!
Johnny	What about?
William Stickers	*[Brandishing a paper]* This!
	Wobbler, Bigmac, and Yo-less gape open-mouthed at what, to them, seems to be a paper floating in mid-air!
Wobbler	Poltergeist! I saw the film! Saucepans flying through the air!
Alderman Bowler	What is the fat boy talking about?
Yo-less	It's just a freak wind!
Bigmac	I can't feel a wind!
Alderman Bowler	What is a poltergeist?
Johnny	Look, will everyone just be quiet! *[To his friends]* Um, look. These, er, people want to talk to us, er, me.
Wobbler	Are they … breath-impaired?
	The lights dim further as night draws in.
Yo-less	Don't be so wet. That sounds like asthma. Come on. If you mean it, say it. Come right out with it. Are they … er *[looking around at the darkening sky]* post-senior citizens?
Wobbler	Are they lurching?

Alderman Bowler	You didn't tell us about this. In the paper. Well, it is called a newspaper, but it has pictures of women in the altogether – which might well be seen by respectable married women and young children!
William Stickers	They're wearing swimming suits.
Alderman Bowler	Swimming suits? But I can see almost all of their legs!
Sylvia Liberty	Nothing wrong with that. Healthy bodies enjoying callisthenics in the God-given sunlight. And very practical clothing, I may say.
Antonio Vicenti	*[Aside, to Johnny]* That's Mrs Sylvia Liberty. Died nineteen fourteen. Tireless suffragette.
Johnny	Suffragette?
Antonio Vicenti	Don't they teach you about these things at school? Suffragettes campaigned for votes for women. They used to chain themselves to railings and chuck eggs at policemen and throw themselves under the Prince of Wales's horse on Derby Days.
Johnny	Wow!
Antonio Vicenti	But Mrs Liberty got the instructions wrong and threw herself under the Prince of Wales. Killed outright. He was a very heavy man, I believe.
Johnny	Who's the man next to her? In the rather old-fashioned football kit.
Antonio Vicenti	Old fashioned? Oh … yes. That's Stanley 'Wrong Way' Roundaway. Used to play for Blackbury Wanderers.
Johnny	Right.
William Stickers	*[Butting in]* It says in this newspaper that the cemetery is going to be closed. Sold. By the council. It's going to be built on.
Johnny	Er, yes. Didn't you know?
William Stickers	Was anyone supposed to tell us?
Bigmac	What're they saying?

Johnny	They're annoyed about the cemetery being sold.
Alderman Bowler	This is our home. What will happen to us, young man?
Johnny	[*To **Alderman Bowler**] Just a minute. Yo-less?
Yo-less	Yes?
Johnny	They want to know what will happen to them if the cemetery's sold off.
Yo-less	I think … that the, er, coffins and that get dug up and put somewhere else. I think there's special places.
Sylvia Liberty	I'm not standing for that! I paid five pounds, seven shillings, and sixpence for my plot! I remember the document distinctly. 'Last resting place', it said. It didn't say 'after eighty years you'll be dug up and moved so the living can build a –' … what does it say?
William Stickers	Modern purpose-designed offices. Whatever that means.
Johnny	I think it means they were designed on purpose.
William Stickers	That's the living for you. No thought for the downtrodden masses.
Johnny	Well, according to the paper the council says it costs too much to keep up, and the land's worth more for building on … Look, it's not my fault. I like this place, too.
Alderman Bowler	So what are you going to do about it?
Johnny	Me? Why me?
Sylvia Liberty	You can see and hear us.
William Stickers	So you must go and tell the council that we … aren't … going … to … move!
Johnny	They won't listen to me! I'm only twelve! I can't even vote!
William Stickers	Yes, but *we're* over twenty-one. Technically, I mean.
Antonio Vicenti	Yes, but we're dead.

Alderman Bowler	I served this city faithfully for over fifty years. I do not see why I should lose my vote just because I'm dead.
Johnny	Well … I'll see what I can do.
Alderman Bowler	Good man. And we'd like a paper delivered every day.
Antonio Vicenti	No, no. It's hard to turn the pages.
Johnny	I'll think of something. Something better than newspapers.
William Stickers	Right. And you'll tell these council people that we're not going to take this lying down!
	*The Dead drift off stage. **Stanley 'Wrong Way' Roundaway** initially drifts off the wrong way, but is rounded up by a couple of the other **Dead** and goes off with the others. There is a pause.*
Wobbler	Have they gone?
Yo-less	Not that they were here.
Johnny	They were here. And now they've gone. Let's go. I need to think. They want me to stop this place being built on.
Yo-less	We'll help.
Wobbler	Will we? It's meddlin' with the occult. Your mum'll go spare.
Yo-less	No. It's a Christian cemetery. So it's helping Christian souls. That's OK.
Johnny	I think there's a Jewish part of the cemetery.
Bigmac	That's all right. Jewish is the same as Christian.
Yo-less	Er … not quite, but near enough. We've got to stick up for Johnny. We stuck up for Bigmac when he was in juvenile court.
Bigmac	It was a political crime.
Yo-less	You stole the Minister of Education's car when she was opening the school!
Bigmac	It wasn't stealing. I meant to give it back.
Yo-less	You drove it into a wall. You couldn't even give it back on a shovel.

Bigmac	Oh, so it's my fault the brakes were faulty. I could've been badly hurt, right?
Yo-less	Anyway. We were behind you, right?
Wobbler	Wouldn't like to have been in front of him!
Yo-less	The point I'm making, is you've got to help your friends, right?
Wobbler/Bigmac	Yeah.
Johnny	I'm touched.
Wobbler	Probably. But we'll still help you.
	Yo-less, Wobbler, and Bigmac exit. Blackout.

SCENE 4

Grandad's house. Grandad is sitting in an armchair, reading the local paper. Johnny walks in and sits on a stool by the chair.

Johnny	Grandad?
Grandad	Yes?
Johnny	How famous was William Stickers?
Grandad	Very famous. Very famous man.
Johnny	I couldn't find him in the encyclopaedia. How about Mrs Sylvia Liberty?
Grandad	Who?
Johnny	She was a suffragette.
Grandad	Never heard of her.
Johnny	All right ... how about Mr Antonio Vicenti?
Grandad	What? Old Tony Vicenti? What's he up to now?
Johnny	Was he famous for anything?

Grandad	He ran a joke shop in Alma Street where the multi-storey car park is now. You could buy stink bombs and itching powder. He used to do conjuring tricks at kids' parties.
Johnny	Was he a famous man?
Grandad	All the kids knew him. Prisoner of war in Germany he was. But he escaped. Always escaping from things, he was.
Johnny	He wore a carnation pinned to his coat.
Grandad	That's right! Every day. Never saw him without one. Haven't seen him around for years.
Johnny	Grandad? You know that little transistor radio? The one you said was too fiddly and not loud enough?
Grandad	What about it?
Johnny	Can I have it? It's … for some friends. They're quite old. And a bit shut in.
Grandad	Yeah. All right.

*Grandad freezes as **Johnny** steps forward to address the audience. As **Johnny** speaks, the lights fade out on **Grandad**.*

Johnny	I took the radio down to the cemetery and left it for them. I also made some notes about the people who were in there: Alderman Bowler, Mrs Liberty, Mr Stickers – and a quiet, overgrown little grave in one corner; just a flat stone on the ground – just saying *[taking a notebook from his pocket and consulting it]* 'Eric Grimm 1885–1927'. No 'Just Resting', no 'Deeply Missed', not even 'Died', although probably he had. The next day, we all went down to the library …

Blackout.

SCENE 5

*The library. **Yo-less**, **Bigmac**, and **Wobbler** are onstage, looking at copies of old papers. **Johnny** enters.*

Johnny	Found anyone famous yet? Nearly everyone who's died around here is buried in that cemetery. If we can find someone famous, that'll make it a famous place. There's a cemetery in London that's only famous cos Karl Marx is buried there.
Bigmac	Karl Marx? What's he famous for?
Wobbler	You're really ignorant, you are. Karl Marx. He was the one with the curly blond hair and the carhorn. You know, the one that never spoke.
Yo-less	No, he was the one that used to *[adopting an awful Italian accent]* talk-a like-a that-a.
Johnny	Oh, ha-ha-ha! Very funny. He was not one of the Marx Brothers.
Yo-less	Yeah. We know.
Bigmac	So what films was he in, then?
Wobbler	What did you say the Alderman was called?
Johnny	Thomas Bowler. Why?
Wobbler	It says here that he got the council to build a memorial horse-trough in the square in nineteen hundred and five. It came in useful very quickly too, it says here.
Johnny	Why?
Wobbler	Well … it says here, the next day the first motor car ever to drive into Blackbury crashed into it and caught fire. They used the water to put the fire out. The council praised Alderman Bowler for his forward thinking.
Yo-less	Forward thinking? Building a horse-trough when motor cars had just been invented?

Wobbler	Let's face it, this is a town where famous people don't come from.
Yo-less	*[Looking at another paper]* It says here, that Addison Vincent Fletcher of Alamo Terrace invented a form of telephone in nineteen twenty-two.
Wobbler	Oh great. But phones had been invented years before that.
Yo-less	It says, he said his one was better.
Wobbler	Oh yes. *[Dialing on an imaginary phone]* Hello? Is that … *[pausing to ask the others]* who invented the telephone?
Yo-less	Thomas Edison?
Bigmac	Sir Humphrey Telephone.
Johnny	Alexander Graham Bell. *[To Bigmac]* Sir Humphrey Telephone?
Wobbler	Hello, Mr Bell. You know that telephone you invented years ago? Well mine's better. And I'm just off to discover America – but I'm discovering it better.
Bigmac	That makes sense, actually. No point in discovering a place until there's proper hotels and stuff.
Wobbler	It's impossible for anyone famous to come from round here, because everyone round here is mental!
Yo-less	Got one.
Bigmac	Who? Which one?
Yo-less	The footballer. Stanley 'Wrong Way' Roundaway. He played for Blackbury Wanderers.
Johnny	I saw him. At the cemetery.
Bigmac	Any good?
Wobbler	*[Looking over Yo-less's shoulder]* Says he scored a record number of goals.
Bigmac	Sounds good.

Wobbler	Own goals.
Yo-less	Greatest number of own goals in the history of any sport, it says. He kept getting over-excited and losing his sense of direction. But he was a good footballer, apart from that, it says. *[Picking up another paper]* Now – look at this.
Wobbler	What?
Yo-less	This is from nineteen sixteen. They're all going off to war. The First World War. Says here, it was the Blackbury Old Pals Battalion. There's a photo of them all in the paper. They all joined up at the same time …

*The lights dim on everyone but **Johnny**, who looks thoughtful. There is a sound of orders being shouted, of machine-gun fire. The lights go up again.*

Yo-less	… and look, here's a paper from a month or so later. It lists all the local men killed at … the Somme. Let's check them against the photo in that paper.

*Yo-less, **Johnny**, **Bigmac**, and **Wobbler** pour over the two newspapers. There is a moment's silence as their eyes move from one paper to the other. The horror of the losses slowly dawns on them.*

Johnny	*[Shocked]* They all died. Four weeks after this photo was taken. All of them.

Yo-less scans the list of dead soldiers and then looks at the photograph again.

Yo-less	Wait a minute … except for Atkins, T. He didn't die. It also says here that a Pals Battalion was when people all from one town or even one street could all join the army together if they wanted, and all get sent to … the same place.
Bigmac	But … four weeks?
Wobbler	Yes, but you're always going on about joining the army.
Bigmac	Well … yeah … war, yeah. Proper fighting, with M16s and stuff. Not just all going off grinning and getting shot.

Yo-less	They all marched off together because they were friends, and got killed.
Johnny	Except for Atkins, T. I wonder what happened to him?
Yo-less	It was nineteen sixteen. If he's still alive, he'll be dead. Perhaps he came back from the war and moved somewhere else.
Bigmac	It would've been a bit lonely round here, after all …

They all look at him

Sorry.

The lights fade down on them.

• •

SCENE 6

*The lights come up on the cemetery where **Alderman Bowler**, **Sylvia Liberty**, **Antonio Vicenti**, **William Stickers**, **Solomon Einstein**, **Stanley 'Wrong Way' Roundaway**, **Addison Vincent Fletcher**, and **Eric Grimm** are listening to the radio.*

Radio announcer	*[Off]* … and that brings to an end our programmes for this evening on BBC Radio Blackbury. We'll now hand you back to Radio 2. Goodnight, everyone.

Solomon Einstein leans forward and switches off the radio.

Addison Vincent Fletcher	So that's wireless telegraphy, is it? Hah! So much for Count Alice Radioni!
Antonio Vicenti	Radioni? It was Marconi who invented the radio.
Addison Vincent Fletcher	Yes, but who do you think he stole the idea from?
Antonio Vicenti	Good grief! Who cares who invented it? Did you hear what the living are planning? They're going to steal our cemetery!
Alderman Bowler	Yes, but I didn't know all this was going on, did you? All this music and … the things they were talking about! Who

is Shakespeare's Sister and why is she singing on the wireless? What is a Batman? And they said the last prime minister was a woman! That can't be right! Women can't even vote.

Antonio Vicenti	Yes, they can.
Sylvia Liberty	Hurrah!
Alderman Bowler	Well, they couldn't in *my* time!
William Stickers	There's so much we don't know.
Antonio Vicenti	So – why don't we find out?
William Stickers	How?
Antonio Vicenti	A man on the wireless said that you can ring the wireless station on the telephone to 'discuss problems that affect us all today'. A 'phone-in' programme, he said.
William Stickers	Well?
Antonio Vicenti	There's a phone box out in the street.
Alderman Bowler	But how would we work the machinery?
Addison Vincent Fletcher	Oh, I'm sure Mr Einstein and I will be able to sort it out. After all, it's just a less refined version of my own invention, mm?
Sylvia Liberty	Well, come on then!

Eric Grimm clears his throat. **The Dead** *all turn and look at him.*

Eric Grimm	You can't go outside. You know that's wrong.
Alderman Bowler	Only a little way, Eric. That can't do any harm. It's for the good of the …
Eric Grimm	It's wrong!
Antonio Vicenti	We don't have to listen to him.
Eric Grimm	You'll get into terrible trouble.
Antonio Vicenti	No, we won't.
Eric Grimm	It's dabbling with the 'known'. You'll all get into terrible trouble and it won't be my fault. You are bad people.

Eric Grimm turns and walks back to his grave.

Sylvia Liberty	Come on!
William Stickers	Yes, but … that's … outside …
Antonio Vicenti	Not far outside.
Alderman Bowler	Yes, but …
Antonio Vicenti	The little boy stood in front of us and talked to us. And he was so frightened. And we can't walk six feet?
William Stickers	It's all right for you, Vicenti, you spent most of your life escaping from things! But this is our place! This is where we belong!
Antonio Vicenti	It's only a few steps …

The Dead start to make their way out of the cemetery (as before, Stanley 'Wrong Way' Roundaway starts to exit the wrong way to all the rest, but is brought back by one of the others).

• •

SCENE 7

*The shopping mall. BBC Radio Blackbury is blaring out of the mall's sound system. **Wobbler**, **Bigmac**, **Johnny**, and **Yo-less** are sitting on a bench, eating burgers out of CFC-free styrofoam boxes.*

Wobbler	Hey, d'you think I could get a job at the burger bar?
Bigmac	No chance. The manager'd take one look at you and see where the profits would go.
Wobbler	Are you saying I'm fat?
Yo-less	Gravitationally enhanced. Anyway, there's loads of people want jobs there. You have to have three A-levels.
Wobbler	What? Just to sell burgers?
Bigmac	No other jobs around. They're shutting all the factories round here. No one's making anything any more.

Wobbler	Well, how does all the stuff get in the shops, then?
Bigmac	That's all made in Taiwanaland or somewhere. That's right, eh? Johnny?
Johnny	What?
Bigmac	You've just been staring at nothing, you know that? You OK?
Johnny	What? Oh, yeah, I'm OK.
Wobbler	He's upset about them dead soldiers.
Yo-less	Look … that's all in the past, right? It's a shame they died, but … well, they'd be dead by now anyway, wouldn't they? It's just history. It's got nothing to do with now.
Johnny	*[Unconvinced]* Right. Maybe. *[Snapping out of it]* What CD did you get, Yo-less?
Yo-less	*[Pulling his CD out of the store bag]* 'Famous British Brass Bands'. Excellent.
Wobbler	'Famous British Brass Bands'!?
Yo-less	It's a good one. It's got the old Blackbury Rubber Boot Factory Band playing the 'Floral Dance'. Very famous piece.
Wobbler	You're just basically not black, are you? I'm going to report you to the Rastafarians.
Yo-less	*You* like reggae and blues.
Wobbler	That's different …

Over the speakers we now hear **The Dead's** *phone conversation with Radio Blackbury. All the boys can hear the radio programme, and react to it.*

Sylvia Liberty	*[Off]* Hello? Hello? This is Mrs Sylvia Liberty talking on the electric telephone! Hello? I demand to be heard this instant!
DJ	*[Off]* Er, hi. The caller on line … well, er, on *all* the lines, actually …

Sylvia Liberty	*[Off]* You listen to me young man! And don't cut me off to start playing any more phonograph cylinders! Innocent citizens are being evicted from their homes! No account is being taken of their many years of valued service to the community, merely because of an accident of birth …
William Stickers	*[Off, singing to the tune of 'The Red Flag']* The people's shroud is deepest black...
Sylvia Liberty	*[Off]* Will you get off the line, you dreadful Bolshevik! You're nothing but a …

The voices are cut off and, seconds later, music plays over the radio.

Wobbler	You get some real loonies on those phone-ins. You ever listen to 'Mad Jim's Late-Night Explosion'?
Yo-less	He's not mad, he just says he is. All he does is play old records and go 'yeah!' and 'yowsahyowsah!' a lot. That's not mad. That's pathetic.
Wobbler	Yes.
Bigmac	Yes.
Yo-less	Yes.

*They look at **Johnny**. They all know the voices were not the usual radio loonies.*

Yo-less	Er … that was *them*, wasn't it?
Johnny	Yes. It was them.
Yo-less	How can they use the phone?
Johnny	I don't know. I suppose some of them knew how to use it when they were alive. And maybe being dead's like … electricity or something.
Wobbler	Who was the one singing?
Johnny	That was William Stickers. He's a bit of a communist.
Yo-less	I didn't think there were any communists left these days.

Johnny	There aren't. And he's one of them.
Yo-less	I think you've started something. Giving them that radio.
Johnny	That's what I think too. Look, I've got to go. I'm supposed to be going with my mum to visit my grandmother.

Johnny exits. Lights down.

SCENE 8

*An old people's home. **Johnny**, **Johnny's Mum**, **Johnny's Gran**, and **Grandad** sit in a semicircle. There are a few seconds of silence, before **Johnny** turns to the audience and speaks. A couple of old people shuffle past at random during **Johnny's** speech.*

Johnny	It's not that Sunshine Acres is a bad place. It's clean enough and the staff seem OK. But somehow it's more gloomy than the cemetery. It's the way everyone shuffles around quietly, or sits around waiting for their next meal, just because there's nothing else to do. It's like … life hasn't stopped yet and being dead hasn't started, so all you have to do is hang around. Every week we come here, have the same conversation, and go again. Except that this week, I noticed that on one of the rooms the name was Mr T. Atkins.

*A **Nurse** enters carrying a cardboard box. **Johnny** stands up and intercepts her.*

Johnny	Excuse me.
Nurse	Yes?
Johnny	I thought, you know, I might drop in and have a chat with Mr Atkins. Er … I'm doing a project at school – about the Blackbury Pals.
Nurse	A project? Oh, well that's different then. The Blackbury Pals?
Johnny	They were … some soldiers. Mr Atkins was one of them, I think. Uh … where … ?

Nurse	I'm really sorry, but I'm afraid he passed away yesterday, dear. Nearly ninety-seven, I think he was. Did you know him?
Johnny	Not … really.
Nurse	He was here for years. He was a nice old man. He used to say that when he died, the war would be over. It was his joke. He used to show us his old army pay book. *[Drawing it from the box]* Look. 'Tommy Atkins,' he'd say. 'I'm the one, I'm the boy, when I'm gone it's all over.'
Johnny	What did he mean?
Nurse	I don't know. This was his stuff. I expect it's all right for you to see, as it's a project. No one ever visited him, except Mr Atterbury from the British Legion. They've asked for his medals, you know.

She gives Johnny the box. He peers into it.

Johnny	A pipe, a tobacco tin, and a huge penknife. Scrap book. A box …

He sits down, takes out the box, and opens it.

… with some medals in it.

He puts it back.

A photograph …

He takes out a photo. It is a print of the photo that had been in the paper, a group photograph of all the Pals. He turns it over and reads the back.

'Old comrades! We're the boys, Kaiser Bill! If you know a better 'ole, go to it!' They've all signed it. All of them. And under every name – except Mr Atkins's – there's a pencilled cross.

Nurse	What's that, dear?
Johnny	This photograph. They all signed it.
Nurse	Yes. That was him, in the Great War. He used to talk about them a lot.
Johnny	Yes.
Nurse	His funeral's on Monday. At the crem. One of us will be there. Well, he was a nice old man.
Johnny	Yes.

Johnny stands, looking at the photo, as the lights go down.

• •

SCENE 9

William Stickers is in a phone box just outside the cemetery fence. He is lit by a spotlight.

Mad Jim	*[Off]* … yowsahyowsahyowsah! And the next caller on Uncle Mad Jim's bodaaacious problem corner iiis …
William Stickers	William Stickers, Mad Jim.
Mad Jim	*[Off]* Hi, Bill. You sound a bit depressed to me.
William Stickers	It's worse than that. I'm dead, Jim.
Mad Jim	*[Off]* Wow! I can see that could be a real downer, Bill. Care to tell us about it?
William Stickers	You sound very understanding, comrade. Well … events seem to have passed me by. I mean, how is Stalin managing in the glorious Soviet Union?
Mad Jim	*[Off]* Seems to me you haven't been keeping up with current events, Bill.
William Stickers	I thought I'd explained about that.
Mad Jim	*[Off]* Oh, right. You've been dead, right? You better now?

William Stickers	It's not something you get better from, Jim.
Mad Jim	*[Off]* So, tell us, Bill, what's it like … being dead?
William Stickers	Like? Like? It is extremely *dull*.
Mad Jim	*[Off]* Oh dear, oh dear. Well, look, for Bill and all the other dead people out there, here's one from the vaults by Michael Jackson – 'Thriller' …

*As the music starts, **The Dead** – including **Alderman Bowler**, **Sylvia Liberty**, **Antonio Vicenti**, **Solomon Einstein**, and **Addison Vincent Fletcher** drift onto the stage and join in with the dance.*

*Stanley 'Wrong Way' Roundaway, of course, faces upstage – the opposite of all the others! **William Stickers** joins them.*

Alderman Bowler	*[Moonwalking backwards across the stage]* This is how you do it, apparently. Johnny showed me.
Sylvia Liberty	It certainly is a syncopated rhythm. Like this, you say? *[She joins in]*
Alderman Bowler	That's right. And apparently you spin around with your arms out and shout 'Ow!'. Get down and – what was it the man on the wireless said?
Sylvia Liberty	Bogey, I believe.

*For a while, **The Dead** dance around, vaguely in the manner of Michael Jackson's 'Thriller'. After a moment or two, **Johnny** rushes on.*

Johnny	You shouldn't be doing this!
Antonio Vicenti	Why not?
Johnny	It's the middle of the night!
Antonio Vicenti	Well? We don't sleep!
Johnny	I mean … what would your descendants think?
Sylvia Liberty	Serve them right for not visiting us! We're making carpets!

William Stickers	Cutting a rung!
Alderman Bowler	A rug. Cutting a rug. That's what Mr Benbow, who died in nineteen forty-one, says it is called. Getting down and bogeying.

The music stops.

Sylvia Liberty	That was extremely enjoyable. Mr Fletcher! Mr Einstein! Be so good as to instruct the wireless man to play something more!

Addison Vincent Fletcher and Solomon Einstein cross to the phone box and start to tinker. Johnny goes across to see what they are doing.

Solomon Einstein	Hello, Johnny. I don't think ve've met before. Solomon Einstein: eighteen sixty-nine to nineteen thirty-two.
Johnny	Like Albert Einstein?
Solomon Einstein	He vas my distant cousin. Relatively speaking.

Solomon Einstein and Addison Vincent Fletcher laugh.

Johnny	Who're you ringing up?
Addison Vincent Fletcher	Well, we were going to call back the radio station, but I was just having a look at the world.
Johnny	What's going on? You said you couldn't leave the cemetery!
Antonio Vicenti	No one has explained this to you? They do not teach you in schools?
Johnny	Well, we don't get lessons in dealing with gho … with dead people, I mean. Sorry.
Antonio Vicenti	We're not ghosts, Johnny. We're something else. But now you see us and hear us, we're free. You're giving us what we don't have.
Johnny	What's that?
Antonio Vicenti	I can't explain. But while you're thinking of us, we're free.

Eric Grimm appears at the other side of the cemetery fence.

Eric Grimm	Send him away.
Johnny	Who's that?
Antonio Vicenti	Mr Grimm.
Johnny	Oh yes. I couldn't find anything about him in the paper.
Antonio Vicenti	I'm not surprised. In those days, there were things they didn't put in.
Eric Grimm	You go away, boy. You're meddling with things you don't understand. You're imperilling your immortal soul. And theirs. You go away, you bad boy.
	He walks off.
Antonio Vicenti	Anyway, how are you? Are you doing anything tomorrow? We're all going to a funeral.
Johnny	Mr Atkins?
Antonio Vicenti	*[Surprised]* Yes.
Johnny	I'll be there.
	The lights go down.

• •

SCENE 10

*The cemetery chapel. **Johnny** and **The Dead** are at Mr Atkins's funeral. Also there are the **Nurse** and **Mr Atterbury** of the British Legion. The living are at the front of the chapel, with **The Dead** in the pews behind them. We can hear a bit of organ music, as the service comes to an end. **Johnny** turns around and whispers to **Addison Vincent Fletcher**, behind him.*

Johnny	Why are you here?
Addison Vincent Fletcher	It's allowed. We used to go to all the funerals in the cemetery. Help them settle in. It's always a bit of a shock.

Johnny	Oh.
Addison Vincent Fletcher	And seeing as we knew you were going to be here, we thought we should make the effort. Mr Vicenti said it was worth a try. We're getting better at it!

The service ends. All rise. **The Dead** *leave smartly, followed by the* **Nurse** *(as usual,* **Stanley 'Wrong Way' Roundaway** *has to be helped out the correct way!).* **Mr Atterbury,** *carrying Tommy Atkins's medal box, starts to leave, but is stopped by* **Johnny.**

Johnny	Excuse me? Are you Mr … Atterbury? From the British Legion?
Mr Atterbury	Yes, lad.
Johnny	My name's Johnny Maxwell.
Mr Atterbury	And I'm Ronald Atterbury. How do you do?
Johnny	Are those Mr Atkins's medals?
Mr Atterbury	Yes, son. The lady from the home said you're doing a project?
Johnny	Um. Yes. Can I ask you some stuff?
Mr Atterbury	Of course, yes.

Johnny *and* **Mr Atterbury** *sit down on a bench.*

Johnny	Well, when Mr Atkins said that he was 'the one' … um. Well, I know about the Blackbury Pals, how they all got killed apart from him. But I don't think that's what he meant.
Mr Atterbury	You know about the Pals, do you?
Johnny	Yes. From the local paper.
Mr Atterbury	But you don't know about Tommy Atkins? Why he was so proud of the name?
Johnny	No. No, I don't.
Mr Atterbury	You see … in the Great War, the First World War … when a new recruit joined the army he had to fill in his pay book, yes? Name and address and that sort of thing? And to help them do

it, the army did a kind of guide to how to fill it in. And on the guide, where it said 'name', they put 'Tommy Atkins'. It was just a name. Just to show them that that's where their name should be, but it became a sort of joke. Tommy Atkins came to mean the average soldier …

Johnny	Like the 'man in the street'?

A sound of marching feet can be heard in the distance, and a military band playing 'Tipperary'. The lights start to dim. **Private Atkins, T.** *enters and stands to attention.*

Mr Atterbury	Yes. Very much like that. Tommy Atkins, the British Tommy.
Johnny	So … in a way … *all* soldiers were Tommy Atkins?
Mr Atterbury	Yes, I suppose you could put it like that. Rather fanciful, of course. The army used it because it was a common sort of name. I know our Mr Atkins was very proud of it. He was a strange old boy. I used to see him regularly at …

The Blackbury Pals march on (through the audience?). They look straight ahead, marching in slow motion, almost. As they pass **Tommy Atkins,** *he joins them. They turn and march off the way they came.* **Johnny** *sees all this, but no one else does.*

Johnny	He's going back to France.
Mr Atterbury	What?
Johnny	Tommy Atkins. He's going back.
Mr Atterbury	How did you know that?
Johnny	Uh …
Mr Atterbury	I expect the lady from the home told you, mm? Yes, we're taking him back this week. He gave us a map reference. Very precise, too. We'll scatter his ashes there.
Johnny	Where … the Pals died?
Mr Atterbury	That's right. He was always talking about them.
Johnny	Sir?

Mr Atterbury	Yes?
Johnny	There was a Sergeant Atterbury in the Pals. Are you related to him?
Mr Atterbury	*[Surprised]* Yes. He was my father. I never knew him. He married my mother before he went off to war.
Johnny	Can I ask you one more question?
Mr Atterbury	Yes.
Johnny	Mr Atkins's medals. Were they, you know, for anything special?
Mr Atterbury	They were campaign medals. Soldiers got them, really, just for being there.
Johnny	Yes. Sometimes being there is all you can do.

Johnny starts to leave. Mr Atterbury stays on the bench, staring ahead. Johnny pauses, looks at Mr Atterbury, and seems about to go back to him, when Antonio Vicenti enters.

Antonio Vicenti	No.
Johnny	I was only going to …
Antonio Vicenti	What … ? To tell him you'd seen them? What good would that do? Perhaps he's seeing them, too. Inside his head.
Johnny	Well …
Antonio Vicenti	It wouldn't work.

A short pause.

They'll start taking us out of the cemetery the day after tomorrow, you know.

Johnny	I'm sorry. I wish there was something I could do.
Antonio Vicenti	There still might be.

Johnny and Antonio Vicenti exit. Lights out.

SCENE 11

The Dead are gathered on the canal bank, in front of a battered old TV set (its back is to the audience, so that all we can see is the glow its screen casts on The Dead). Eric Grimm stands to one side, watching from the other side of the cemetery fence. Johnny enters.

Johnny	What's happened? Why are you all here on the canal bank?
Antonio Vicenti	You know that old television set that had been dumped here? They made it work.
Johnny	But how … ? I mean, the screen was smashed …
Addison Vincent Fletcher	Another successful marriage of advanced theoretics and practical know-how, eh, Mr Einstein?
Solomon Einstein	A shtep in ze right direction, Mr Fletcher.
Johnny	Oh. I see. It's the ghost of the television!
Solomon Einstein	Vot a clever boy!
Addison Vincent Fletcher	But with improvements.
Johnny	There's an old motor car, a Ford Capri, in the canal somewhere along there. Wobbler saw some men dumping it. D'you think you could make that work, too?
Addison Vincent Fletcher	I shall see to it directly. The internal combustion engine could certainly do with some improvements.

Johnny	But, look. Machines aren't alive, so how can they have ghosts?
Solomon Einstein	But zey haf existence. From moment to moment. Zo, ve find ze right moment, yes?
Johnny	Sounds a bit occult.
Solomon Einstein	No! It is physics! It is *beyond* physics. It is … *meta*physics. From the Greek *meta*, meaning 'beyond', and *physika*, meaning … er …
Antonio Vicenti	Physics.
Solomon Einstein	Exactly!
Johnny	Nothing finishes. Nothing's ever really over.
Addison Vincent Fletcher	Correct! Are you a physicist?
Johnny	Me? I don't know anything about science!
Solomon Einstein	Marvellous! Ideal qualification!
Addison Vincent Fletcher	Ignorance is important. It is an absolutely vital part of the learning process!
Eric Grimm	There will be trouble because of this. This is disobedience. Meddling with the physical.
	Johnny crosses to him.
Eric Grimm	There'll be trouble. And it will be *your* fault, John Maxwell. You're getting them excited. Is this any way for the dead to behave?
Johnny	Mr Grimm?
Eric Grimm	Yes?
Johnny	Who are you?
Eric Grimm	That's none of your business.
Johnny	I didn't mean to …
Eric Grimm	No good will come of it.

Johnny	Look, I'd better be getting home for my tea.
	Johnny and *The Dead* *exchange waves, and he leaves.*
Addison Vincent Fletcher	The principle is astonishingly simple. A tiny point of light, that's all it is. Whizzing backwards and forwards inside a glass bottle. Much easier to control than sound waves …
Sylvia Liberty	Excuse me. When you stand in front of the screen you make the picture go blurred.
Addison Vincent Fletcher	Sorry. What's happening now?
William Stickers	Mr McKenzie has told Dawn that Janine can't go to Doraleen's party.
Alderman Bowler	I must say, I thought Australia was a bit different. More kangaroos and fewer young women in unsuitable clothing.
William Stickers	I'm quite happy with the young women!
Sylvia Liberty	Mr Stickers! For shame! You're dead!
William Stickers	But I have a very good memory, Mrs Liberty.
	The 'Cobbers' theme tune can be heard. The lights dim. It is starting to get dark.
Solomon Einstein	Oh, is it over? But zere iss ze mystery of who took ze money from Mick's coat!
Sylvia Liberty	The man in the television said there would be another performance tomorrow night.
Antonio Vicenti	It is getting dark. Time we were getting back.
	Pause.
	If we want to go, that is.
Alderman Bowler	Well, I'm blowed if I'm going back in there!
Sylvia Liberty	Thomas Bowler!
Alderman Bowler	Well, if a man can't swear when he's dead, it's a poor look-out. Blowed, blowed, blowed. And damn. I mean, there's all sorts of

	things going on. I don't see why we should go back in there. It's dull. No way.
Sylvia Liberty	'No way'?
William Stickers	That's Australian for 'certainly not'.
Sylvia Liberty	But staying where we're put is proper.
Eric Grimm	Ahem.

The Dead look embarrassed, as if they have been caught doing something naughty.

Eric Grimm	I entirely agree.
Alderman Bowler	Oh. Hello, Eric.
Eric Grimm	Will you listen to what you're saying? You're dead. Act your age. It's over. You know what will happen if you leave. You know what will happen if you're too long away. What happens if the day comes and you're not here? The Day of Judgement. We must be ready. Not gallivanting off apeing your juniors. Not dabbling with the 'ordinary'.
Alderman Bowler	Well, I've waited eighty years. If it happens tonight, it happens. I'm going to go and have a look around. Anyone else coming?
William Stickers	Yes. Me.
Alderman Bowler	Anyone else?

Antonio Vicenti and Stanley 'Wrong Way' Roundaway put up their hands.

Eric Grimm	You will get lost! Something will go wrong! And then you'll be wandering forever, and you'll … forget.
Alderman Bowler	There's a world out there, and we helped to make it, and now I want to find out what it's like.
Antonio Vicenti	Besides, if we stick together no one will forget who they are, and we'll all go further.
Sylvia Liberty	Well, if you insist on going, I suppose someone with some sense should accompany you.

Alderman Bowler, William Stickers, Antonio Vicenti, and Sylvia Liberty exit (again, one of them has to rescue Stanley 'Wrong Way' Roundaway and point him in the right direction). This leaves Addison Vincent Fletcher and Solomon Einstein watching the TV, and Eric Grimm observing from over the fence.

Addison Vincent Fletcher	What's got into them? They're acting almost alive.
Eric Grimm	It is disgusting.
Solomon Einstein	On ze other hand ... zere voz a nice little pub in Cable Street.
Addison Vincent Fletcher	You wouldn't get a drink, Solly. They don't serve spirits.

They both laugh.

Solomon Einstein	I used to like it in there. After a hard day stuffing foxes. It voz nice to relax of an evenink.

*They look at each other, nod, and exit for the pub. **Eric Grimm** is left alone as the lights fade to blackout.*

• •

SCENE 12

*The civic centre. **Johnny** enters and addresses the audience. As he speaks, behind him, people are filing into rows of chairs in front of a table on a raised platform. The audience includes **Yo-less**, **Wobbler**, **Bigmac**, **Grandad**, the **Nurse**, **Mr Atterbury**, and others. Everyone has a sheet of paper – a handout from the council. Then **Ms Liberty**, **Mr Bowler** (from United Amalgamated Consolidated Holdings), and a couple of other people take their places at the top table. **Ms Liberty**, in mime, makes her introductory address to the meeting.*

Johnny	The following night there was a public meeting at the civic centre to discuss United Amalgamated Consolidated Holdings' plans for the canal bank, boot factory site, and cemetery. Quite

a few people went. Even some of our teachers. Which is funny, cos you don't really think of them having a real life outside school. The lady from the council was called Ms Liberty; I s'pose she's a descendant of 'our' Mrs Liberty, but it's not really the sort of thing you could ask. There was also a man from United Amalgamated Consolidated Holdings.

Johnny makes his way to the rows of seats and sits down.

Johnny	The meeting started off with Ms Liberty speaking to us, at great length, about nothing in particular …

Ms Liberty's voice now becomes audible as we catch the end of her speech.

Ms Liberty	… providing a better future for the young people of Blackbury. And in the final analysis, it is not even a particularly fine example of Edwardian funeral architecture. And of course, full account of residents' views has been taken at every stage of the planning process. Now then, I would like to invite Mr Bowler from United Amal –

Johnny stands.

Johnny	Excuse me, please?
Ms Liberty	*[Dismissively]* Questions at the end, please.
Johnny	When is the end, please? Only I have to be in bed by ten.
Mr Atterbury	Let the lad ask his question. He's doing a project.
Grandad	Here, here.
Ms Liberty	*[A little ungraciously]* Oh … very well. What was it, young man?
Johnny	Um, well, the thing is … the thing I want to know is … is there anything that anyone can say here, tonight, that's going to make any difference?
Ms Liberty	*[Severely]* That hardly seems an appropriate sort of question.
Mr Atterbury	Seems damned good to me. Why doesn't Mr Bowler from United Amalgamated Consolidated Holdings answer the boy? Just a simple answer will do.

Mr Bowler	We shall, of course, take all views very deeply into consideration. And furthermore –
Johnny	But there's a sign up on the site that says you're going to build anyway. Only I don't think many people want the old cemetery built on. So you'll take the sign down, will you?
Mr Bowler	We have in fact bought the –
Johnny	You paid five pence. I'll give you a pound.

The audience laughs.

Yo-less	I've got a question, too.
Ms Liberty	Ah. Yes. Um. We'll, er, take the question from that other young man.

Wobbler rises.

No, not you, the other one. The one with the shirt, er …

Yo-less	*[Helpfully]* The black one. Why did the council sell the cemetery in the first place?
Ms Liberty	I think we have covered that very fully. The cost of upkeep –
Yo-less	But I don't see how there's much upkeep in a cemetery. Sending someone once or twice a year to cut the brambles down doesn't sound like much of a cost to me.
Johnny	We'd do it for nothing.
Wobbler	Would we?
Ms Liberty	The fact, young man, as I have explained time and again, is that it is simply too expensive to maintain a cemetery that is –
Johnny	No. It isn't simply too expensive.
Ms Liberty	How dare you interrupt me!
Johnny	It says in your papers that the cemetery makes a loss. But a cemetery can't make a loss. It's not like a business or something. It just *is*. My friend Bigmac says what you're calling a loss is just the value of the land for building offices.

	It's the council tax you'd get from United Amalgamated Consolidated Holdings. The dead don't pay council tax so they're not worth anything.
Ms Liberty	We are a democratically elected council …
Mr Atterbury	I'd like to raise a few points on that. There are certain things about this sale that I should like to see explained in a more democratic way.
Johnny	I've had a good look round the cemetery. I've been … doing a project. It's full of stuff. It doesn't matter that no one in there is really famous. They were famous *here*. They lived and got on with things and died. They were *people*. It's wrong to think that the past is something that's just gone. It's still there. It's just that *you've* gone past. If you drive through a town, it's still there in the rear-view mirror. Time is a road, but it doesn't roll up behind you. Things aren't over just because they're *past*. Do you see that?
	Pause.
	And … and, if we forget about them, we're just a lot of people living in … in buildings. It's wrong to throw all that away.
Ms Liberty	Nevertheless, we have to deal with the present day. The dead are no longer here and I am afraid they do not vote.
Johnny	You're wrong. They are here and they have got a vote. I've been working it out. In my head. It's called tradition. And they outvote us twenty to one.
	Mr Atterbury *starts to clap. He is soon joined by the rest of the audience. Then he stands, and the applause dies down for him.*
Ms Liberty	Mr Atterbury, sit down. I am running this meeting, you know.
Mr Atterbury	I am afraid this does not appear to be the case. The boy is right. Too much has been taken away, I know that. You dug up the high street. It had a lot of small shops. People lived there. Now it's all walkways and plastic signs and people are afraid of it at night. Afraid of the town where they live! I'd be ashamed of that, if I was you. And we had a coat of arms up on the

town hall. Now all we've got is some plastic logo thing. And you took the allotments and built that shopping mall and all the little shops went out of business. And then you knocked down a lot of houses and built that big tower block where no one wants to live.

Ms Liberty   Now look, I was not on the council then. In any case, it is generally recognized that the Joshua N'Clement tower block was a … misplaced idea.

Mr Atterbury   A bad idea, you mean?

Ms Liberty   Yes, if you must put it like that.

Mr Atterbury   So mistakes can be made, can they?

Ms Liberty   Nevertheless, the plain fact is, that we must build for the future …

Mr Atterbury   I'm very glad to hear you say that, madam chairman, because I'm sure you'll agree that the most successful buildings have got very deep foundations.

There is another round of applause.

Ms Liberty   I feel I have no alternative but to close this meeting. Things are getting out of hand. This was supposed to be an informative occasion.

Mr Atterbury   I think it has been.

Johnny   But you can't close the meeting!

Ms Liberty   Indeed, I can!

Johnny   You can't. Because this is a public hall, and no one's done anything wrong.

Ms Liberty   Then we shall leave, and there really will be no point to the meeting!

Ms Liberty, Mr Bowler, and the others at the table sweep up their papers and storm out, to the accompaniment of a slow handclap and jeers from the audience. When they have gone, there is a silence.

Woman in the audience	Can we actually stop it from happening? It all sounded very official.
Mr Atterbury	Officially, I don't think we can. There was a proper sale.
Grandad	There's plenty of other sites. The old jam works in Slate Road, and all that area where the goods yards used to be.
Woman in the audience	And we could give them their money back.
Johnny	We could give them double their money back.
	There is laughter. **Mr Atterbury** *moves to the raised table and addresses the meeting.*
Mr Atterbury	It seems to me, that a company like United Amalgamated Consolidated Holdings has to take notice of people. Big companies like that don't like fuss. And they don't like being laughed at. And if they thought we were serious … and if we threaten to offer them, yes, double their money back … *[He chuckles]*
Woman in the audience	And then we ought to do something about the high street.
Grandad	And get some decent playgrounds and things, instead of all those 'amenities' all over the place.
Wobbler	And blow up the Joshua N'Clement block and get some proper houses built.
Bigmac	Yo!
Yo-less	Here, here.
Mr Atterbury	One thing at a time. Let's rebuild Blackbury first. We can see about Jerusalem tomorrow. But we ought to find a name for ourselves.
Grandad	The Blackbury Preservation Society?
Mr Atterbury	Sounds like something you put in a jar.
Grandad	The Blackbury Conservation Society.

Mr Atterbury	Still sounds like jam to me.
Johnny	The Blackbury Pals.
Mr Atterbury	It's a good name but … no. Not now. They were officially the Blackbury Volunteers. That's a good name.
Woman in the audience	But it doesn't say what we're going to do, does it?
Johnny	If we start off not knowing what we're going to do, we could do anything.
Mr Atterbury	The Blackbury Volunteers it is, then!

The lights fade. They all exit.

• •

SCENE 13

*A street in Blackbury. **Alderman Bowler**, **William Stickers**, **Sylvia Liberty**, **Antonio Vicenti**, and **Stanley 'Wrong Way' Roundaway** enter.*

Sylvia Liberty	Moving pictures have certainly come a long way since my day. That was a fascinating film.
Alderman Bowler	Well, I think some of those tricks were done with mirrors. They can't really have bred a Tyrannosaurus Rex just for a moving picture.
William Stickers	What should we do now?
Sylvia Liberty	We should be getting back. To the cemetery.
Alderman Bowler	Madam, the night is young!

***Solomon Einstein** and **Addison Vincent Fletcher** enter.*

| Alderman Bowler | Hello, you two. Where did you get to? |
| Addison Vincent Fletcher | The moon. |

William Stickers	What? The moon? What – *[pointing up at the sky]* that moon?
Addison Vincent Fletcher	Yes.
William Stickers	But how?
Solomon Einstein	Ve used a radio telescope. Travelled along ze radio waves.
Addison Vincent Fletcher	Of all the forces in the universe, the hardest to overcome is the force of habit. Gravity was easy-peasy by comparison.
Alderman Bowler	What was it like?
Solomon Einstein	Ve didn't have time to see much, but I don't think I'd like to live zere.
Alderman Bowler	*[Looking up at the shop names]* You know, I certainly don't remember all these shopkeepers from my time. They must have moved in recently. Mr Boots and Mr Mothercare and Mr Spudjulicay.
Sylvia Liberty	Whom?
Antonio Vicenti	Spud-u-like.
Alderman Bowler	Is that how you pronounce it? I thought perhaps he was French. And electric lights all over the place and no horse … *manure* in the streets at all.
Sylvia Liberty	Really! Please remember you are in the presence of a lady!
William Stickers	That's why he said *manure*.
Alderman Bowler	Shops full of cinematography televisions! Bright colours everywhere! The people seem taller, and they all seem to have their own teeth! An age of miracles and wonders!
Antonio Vicenti	The people don't look very happy.
Alderman Bowler	That's just a trick of the light.
Sylvia Liberty	It's been fun. It's a shame we have to go back.
Alderman Bowler	Go back?

Sylvia Liberty	Now then Thomas. I don't want to sound like Eric Grimm, but you know the rules. We have to return. A day will come.
Alderman Bowler	I'm not going back. I've really enjoyed myself. I'm not going back!
William Stickers	Me neither! Down with tyranny!
Sylvia Liberty	We must be ready for the Judgement Day. Supposing it was tomorrow, and we missed it?
Alderman Bowler	Hah! Being dead's not what I expected. I just thought everything would go dark for a moment and then there'd be a man handing out harps. Isn't that what *you* expected?
William Stickers	Not me. Belief in the survival of the spirit after death is a primitive superstition which has no place in a socialist society!
Solomon Einstein	You don't zink that it might be worth reconsidering your opinions in the light of recent events?
William Stickers	Just because I'm still here does not invalidate the general theory.
Alderman Bowler	Anyway, I don't want to go back. I just wish that this night didn't have to end.
Solomon Einstein	*[To Addison Vincent Fletcher]* Shall ve tell zem?
Addison Vincent Fletcher	Times have changed. All that stuff about being home by dawn and not hearing the cock crow. That was all very well when people thought the earth was flat, but now we know different. Dawn is a place as well as a time. It's all relative. It's always night somewhere in the world. As long as we keep moving, we need never see another dawn!
Sylvia Liberty	What on earth do you mean?
Solomon Einstein	On earth, and around earth. One night and one day, forever chasing one another … We just follow the night around the world …
Addison Vincent Fletcher	A night that never comes to an end. All you need is speed.

*The Dead exit. (**Stanley 'Wrong Way' Roundaway** needs showing the way again.) Blackout.*

SCENE 14

*The cemetery. **Johnny** walks on, carrying a ghetto blaster. He addresses the audience.*

Johnny   The campaign's going really well. Listen …

He switches on the radio in the blaster, and we hear the voices.

Mr Bowler   *[Off]* … at every stage, fully sensitive to public opinion in this matter, I can assure you. But there is no doubt that we entered into a proper and legal contract with the local authority.

Radio interviewer   *[Off]* But the Blackbury Volunteers say too much was decided behind closed doors. They say things were never discussed and that no one listened to the local people.

Mr Atterbury   *[Off]* Of course, this is not the fault of United Amalgamated Consolidated Holdings. They have an enviable record of civic service and co-operation with the public. I think what we have here is a genuine mistake rather than any *near-criminal activity*, and we in the Volunteers would be happy to help them in any constructive way and, indeed, possibly even to *compensate* them.

Mr Bowler   *[Off]* Er, I don't think that will be necessary!

Radio interviewer   *[Off]* Tell me, what exactly is it that United Amalgamated Consolidated Holdings *does*?

*Johnny switches off the radio. **Eric Grimm** enters.*

Johnny   Where's everyone else?

Eric Grimm   Haven't come back. Their graves haven't been slept in. That's what happens when people don't listen. Now they're going to fade away. If they don't get back here before dawn, they'll get more and more insubstantial until they forget who they are and fade away completely. It could be Judgement Day tomorrow, and they won't be here. Hah! Serves them right.

Johnny   *[With a sigh]* I don't know where they've gone, but I don't think anything bad's happened to them.

Eric Grimm	Think what you like.
	He starts to exit.
Johnny	Did you know it's Hallowe'en?
Eric Grimm	*[As he exits]* Is it? I shall have to be careful tonight, then.
	***Eric Grimm** exits. **Yo-less** and **Bigmac** run on.*
Bigmac	Hey, Johnny! Look, in the paper! You're a real hero! Look! 'Council Slammed in Cemetery Sale Rumpus'!

Johnny	*[Reading from the paper]* War hero Ronald Atterbury told the Guardian: "There are young people in this town with more sense of history in their little fingers than some adults have in their entire committee-bound bodies".
Yo-less	And did you see over by the main gate? There's a local TV crew and everything. And there's ecologists who think they've found a rare breed of thrush.
Johnny	They've gone.
Bigmac	Gone where?
Johnny	I don't know. Mr Grimm says that if they're away too long, they … they forget who they were … They're just not here.
Bigmac	Then where are they?
Johnny	I don't know!
Bigmac	And it's Hallowe'en, too.
Johnny	I wanted to tell them. I mean, we might win. Now people are here, TV and everything. I wanted to tell them and now they've gone!

Yo-less	We ought to get back. I've got a project to do on projects.
Johnny	I'm going to look for them.
Bigmac	You'll get into trouble when they do the register.
Johnny	*[Vaguely]* I'll say I've been doing something … social.
Yo-less	Johnny? You OK?
Johnny	Yes, I'm OK. You go on back. I'll see you at Wobbler's party tonight.

Bigmac and Yo-less exit, as Mr Atterbury comes on. He is carrying the old radio.

Mr Atterbury	Hello Johnny, exciting day, isn't it? You really started something, you know.
Johnny	I heard you on the radio. You called United Amalgamated Consolidated Holdings public-spirited and co-operative.
Mr Atterbury	Well, they might be. If they've got no choice. They're a bit shifty, but we might just win through. It's amazing what you can do with a kind word. *[Holding up the radio]* Look at this! Just dumped in the cemetery. People have no respect.
Johnny	What are you going to do with it?
Mr Atterbury	I was going to give it to those council men who are clearing the rubbish off the canal bank and dumping it into a skip.
Johnny	Oh. Right.
Mr Atterbury	Well, see you later, then.
Johnny	Yes. Bye.

Mr Atterbury exits. Johnny looks around him.

Johnny	Mr Grimm? Mr Grimm?

Pause.

I know you're here. You can't leave like the others. You have to stay. Because you're a ghost. A real ghost. You're not just hanging around like the rest of them. You're haunting.

Pause.

What did you do? Were you a murderer or something?

Pause.

I'm afraid they're clearing the canal bank. Sorry about the television.

Johnny *pauses again. There is still no response. He turns and exits.*

*Onstage there is a pattern of moving lights as, over the speakers, we hear the voices of **The Dead**.*

Alderman Bowler *[Off]* How far to morning?

Antonio Vicenti *[Off]* Nearly there. We must go back.

Alderman Bowler *[Off]* What?

Antonio Vicenti *[Off]* We owe the boy something. He took an interest. He remembered us.

Solomon Einstein *[Off]* Zat's absolutely correct. Conservation of energy. Besides, he'll be worrying.

Sylvia Liberty *[Off]* Yes, but, if we go now … we'll become like we were, won't we? I can feel the weight of that gravestone now.

Antonio Vicenti *[Off]* We don't have to be frightened of the morning. We don't have to be frightened of anything. Come on.

Blackout.

SCENE 15

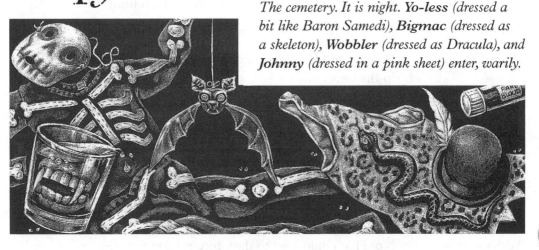

The cemetery. It is night. **Yo-less** *(dressed a bit like Baron Samedi),* **Bigmac** *(dressed as a skeleton),* **Wobbler** *(dressed as Dracula), and* **Johnny** *(dressed in a pink sheet) enter, warily.*

Wobbler	D-did we have to come here on Hallowe'en?
Bigmac	Well, let's face it, your party ran out of steam a bit when everyone decided to go trick or treating round the estate. Now that *would* be scary. Anyway, Johnny said he wanted to come.
Wobbler	Yeah, what are you, Johnny? A gay ghost?
Johnny	Look – Mum washed it with one of Grandad's red vests. It's the only one she'd let me cut a hole in. Anyway, there's nothing wrong with pink. Lots of people wear pink.
Wobbler	Not very spooky, though, is it? Pink?
Johnny	It's not that pink. But what's Yo-less supposed to be?
Yo-less	Baron Samedi, the voodoo god. I got the idea from that James Bond film.
Bigmac	That's racial stereotyping.
Yo-less	No it's not. Not if *I* do it.
Johnny	I'm pretty sure Baron Samedi didn't wear a bowler hat. I'm pretty sure it was a top hat. A bowler hat makes you look like you were off to an office somewhere.

Yo-less	I can't help it. It was all I could get.
Wobbler	Maybe he's Baron Samedi, the voodoo god of chartered accountancy. Anyway, why are we here, Johnny?
Johnny	I wanted to try and get in touch with them again.
Bigmac	Perhaps old Baron Samedi here could use his tarot cards, like in the film.
Yo-less	No. Tarot is European occult. Voodoo is African occult.
Wobbler	How're we supposed to contact the dead, then?
Bigmac	What about the thing with the letters and glasses?
Wobbler	The postman?
Bigmac	You know what I mean.
Yo-less	No. That could lead to dark forces taking over.

Someone coughs offstage.

Yo-less	Listen!
Wobbler	*[Whispering]* What?

There is a clank offstage.

Yo-less	There's someone in the cemetery!
Wobbler	It'll be Johnny's dead pals.
Johnny	No. Wobbler, run back to Mr Atterbury's house over the road and tell him what's happening!
Wobbler	Me? What? By myself?
Johnny	You'll run faster if you're by yourself!
Wobbler	Right!

Wobbler exits. Johnny, Bigmac, and Yo-less peer out towards the audience.

Yo-less	What, exactly, are we doing?

There is the sound of a diesel engine being started up offstage.

Bigmac	Someone's nicking a JCB!
Johnny	I wish that's what they were doing. I reckon someone from United Amalgamated Consolidated Holdings is trying to wreck the cemetery!
Yo-less	Listen, if someone's driving a JCB without lights at this time of night, I'm not hanging around!
	Two lights come on. **Johnny, Bigmac,** *and* **Yo-less** *are illuminated in the headlights of the offstage JCB.*
Johnny	Is that better?
Yo-less	No.
	There is the noise of the machine driving forwards, getting closer.
Johnny	*[Waving his arms in the direction of the machine]* Oi! Stop!
	The engine stops. **Johnny** *whispers to* **Bigmac.**
Johnny	Run away! Quick! Tell someone what's happening!
	Bigmac *runs off. Two men enter, from the audience, and grab* **Johnny** *and* **Yo-less.**
First man	You – are in real trouble, kid.
Second man	Yeah. All this damage to the cemetery …
First man	Which they'll find tomorrow morning …
Second man	Yeah. That's all your fault, that is.
First man	Know what I think? I think it's lucky we happened to be passing and found them messin' around with that JCB, eh? Shame they'd already driven it through the place and wrecked everything. Kids today, eh?
Second man	Yeah, and you'd just better go along with it, cos we know where you live, see?
	Suddenly, as if from nowhere, **Bigmac** *charges on, wielding a length of lead piping. He strikes the first man across the shoulders. In the background, we hear the approaching siren of a police car.*

First man	Hey! What the … ow!

*The **first man** runs off stage. The **second man** releases **Yo-less** in order to try and grab **Bigmac**. **Bigmac** hits him hard across the shins with the pipe. He yells and falls to the floor, holding his damaged shins. **Bigmac** dives onto him and starts to punch him.*

Second man	Ow! Gettim off me!

*Johnny, Bigmac, and Yo-less help to subdue the **second man**. A **police officer** enters holding the **first man**. Another **police officer** enters, with **Wobbler** and **Mr Atterbury**.*

Police officer	*[Lifting the **second man** to his feet]* Right, you. I think you and your friend had better come with us for a nice little ride down to Blackbury nick.

*The **police officers** and the **men** exit.*

Mr Atterbury	Well done, you boys! Well done! I must say, though, I expected a bit more than this from United Amalgamated Consolidated Holdings. I suppose they thought everything would be a lot simpler if the cemetery wasn't worth saving. So they slipped a couple of likely lads a few quid to do … er … a Hallowe'en prank. Come on, I'll give you all a lift home. And then I shall take considerable pleasure in ringing up the chairman of United Amalgamated Consolidated Holdings. *Considerable* pleasure.

Mr Atterbury exits, followed by Yo-less and Bigmac.

Wobbler	Well, that's it. Game over. Let's go home.

Johnny does not move.

Wobbler	Come on.
Johnny	It's not right. It can't end like this.
Wobbler	Best ending. Nasty men foiled. Kids save the day. Everyone gets a sticky bun.
Johnny	No. Something else is going to happen. I've got to go and see. You go with the others.

Wobbler	No argument from me! You sure you'll be OK?
Johnny	Me? Yes, yes, sure. See you tomorrow.
	Wobbler runs off after the others.
Johnny	Something's going to happen.
	Alderman Bowler, Solomon Einstein, Antonio Vicenti, Sylvia Liberty, William Stickers, and Stanley 'Wrong Way' Roundaway enter .
Johnny	You're back!
Antonio Vicenti	Yes. Hello, Johnny.
	We hear the JCB start up again.
Johnny	The JCB? What's happening?
Antonio Vicenti	That's Mr Fletcher.
Johnny	What are you doing?
Alderman Bowler	Isn't this what people wanted? We don't need this place anymore. So if anyone's going to do it, it should be us. That's only right!
	The JCB lights come on again, and the engine noise starts to get louder.
Johnny	But you said this was your place!
Sylvia Liberty	We have left nothing here of any importance.
William Stickers	Force of habit is what has subjugated the working man for too long.
Sylvia Liberty	He's right. We spent far too much time moping around because of what we're not, without any consideration of what we might be. We were trapped in the cemetery because we believed we were trapped. Instead of which, since we aren't encumbered by our bodies, we're even freer to move where we like.
Solomon Einstein	That's right. We're … chronologically gifted.
Alderman Bowler	Dimensionally advantaged.

William Stickers	Bodily unencumbered.
Antonio Vicenti	Enhanced.
Alderman Bowler	So we're off.
Johnny	Where to?
Solomon Einstein	We don't know. But it iss goink to be very interestink to find out.
Johnny	But ... we've saved the cemetery! We had a big meeting! No one's going to build anything on it! Turn the machine off! We've saved the cemetery!
Alderman Bowler	But we don't need it any more. We're dead. We can go where we like!
Johnny	*We* do! We do. We ... need it to be there.
	The engine noise stops.
Solomon Einstein	This iss of course very true. It all balances, you see. The living have to remember. The dead have to forget.
	Addison Vincent Fletcher *walks on.*
Addison Vincent Fletcher	Ah yes, conservation of energy, eh?
Solomon Einstein	Indeed.
Antonio Vicenti	We came to say goodbye. And thank you.
Johnny	I hardly did anything.
Antonio Vicenti	You listened. You tried. You were there. You can get medals just for being there. But now ... we must be somewhere else.
	The Dead *start to drift off.* ***Antonio Vicenti, Alderman Bowler, and Sylvia Liberty*** *remain.*
William Stickers	*[As he goes]* Goodbye, Johnny. Power to the people, eh?
	William Stickers *takes* ***Stanley 'Wrong Way' Roundaway*** *off with him.*

Solomon Einstein	*[As he goes]* Take good care of yourself, Johnny.
Addison Vincent Fletcher	*[As he goes]* Goodbye, Johnny. Thanks for everything.
Johnny	*[To **Antonio Vicenti**]* No … don't go yet. I have to ask you …
Antonio Vicenti	Yes?
Johnny	Um …
Antonio Vicenti	Yes?
Johnny	Are there … angels involved? You know? Or … devils and things? A lot of people would like to know.
Antonio Vicenti	Oh no. I don't think so. That sort of thing … no. That's for the living.
Alderman Bowler	I rather think it's going to be a lot more interesting than that. Mrs Liberty thinks we ought to tell you something. But … it's hard to explain, you know?
Johnny	What is?
Alderman Bowler	By the way, why are you wearing a pink sheet?
Johnny	Um …
Alderman Bowler	I expect it's not important.
Johnny	Yes.
Alderman Bowler	Well. You know those games where this ball runs up and bounces around and ends up in a slot at the bottom?
Johnny	Pinball machines?
Alderman Bowler	Is that what they're called? Right. Well … when you're bouncing around from pin to pin, it is probably very difficult to know that outside the game there's a room and outside the room there's a town and outside the town there's a country and outside the country there's a world, and so on … but it's there, do you see? Once you know about it, you can stop worrying about the slot at the bottom. And you might bounce around a good deal longer.

Johnny	I'll … try to remember it.
Alderman Bowler	Good man. Well, we'd better be going. Goodbye, Johnny.
Sylvia Liberty	Goodbye, Johnny.

Alderman Bowler and Sylvia Liberty exit.

Johnny	Goodbye.
Antonio Vicenti	Well, I think I might as well be off, too.
Johnny	Why, are you all leaving?
Antonio Vicenti	Oh, yes. It's Judgement Day. We decided. It's different for everyone, you see. Enjoy looking after the cemetery. They're places for the living, after all.

*He exits. The lights go down on the cemetery. **Johnny** turns to the audience. He is lit by a spotlight.*

Johnny	So that's how we saved the cemetery. There was a very generous donation to the Blackbury Volunteers from United Amalgamated Consolidated Holdings. As Mr Atterbury said, it's amazing what you can do with a kind word – providing you've also got a big stick. After a few days, I went back to the cemetery.

The lights come up again on the cemetery. It is daytime.

Johnny	Mr Grimm? Mr Grimm?

Eric Grimm enters and sits.

Eric Grimm	Go away. You're dangerous.
Johnny	I thought you'd be a bit … lonely. So I brought you this.

He pulls out a pocket TV.

	It'll work until the batteries die, and then I thought maybe it'd work on ghost batteries.
Eric Grimm	What is it?
Johnny	It's a pocket-sized television. I thought I could hide it right in a bush or somewhere where no one will know except you.

72

Eric Grimm	What are you doing this for?
Johnny	Because I looked you up in the newspaper. May the twenty-first, nineteen twenty-seven. There wasn't very much. Just the bit about them finding … you … in the canal.
Eric Grimm	Oh? Poking around, eh? And what do you think you know about *anything*?
Johnny	Nothing.
Eric Grimm	I don't have to explain.
Johnny	Is that why you couldn't leave with the others?
Eric Grimm	What? I can leave whenever I like. If I'm staying here, it's because I want to.

Johnny moves downstage to address the audience.

Johnny	It wasn't a very long report. It said you were a respectable citizen, then your business failed and there'd been some trouble involving money and then … there'd been the canal. Seems daft to me, because suicide was against the law in those days. So if you failed, you could get locked up in prison to show you that life was really very jolly and thoroughly worth living.

He moves back up to Eric Grimm.

Johnny	You'll be able to turn it on with your mind, I think.
Eric Grimm	Who says I shall want to?

The TV picture comes on and we hear the 'Cobbers' theme.

Johnny	Let's see … you've missed a week … Mrs Swede has just found out that Janine didn't go to the party … Mr Hatt has sacked Jason from the shop because he thinks he took the money …
Eric Grimm	I see.
Johnny	So … I'll be off then, shall I?
Eric Grimm	Right.

Johnny leaves *Eric Grimm* looking at the TV. *Yo-less, Wobbler,* and *Bigmac* enter and stand on the side of the stage. *Johnny* crosses to them.

Yo-less   Was he there?

Johnny   Yes.

Yo-less   What's he doing now?

Johnny   Watching television.

Wobbler   You all right?

Johnny   I was just thinking about the difference between heaven and hell.

Wobbler   That doesn't sound like 'all right' to me.

Johnny   I was thinking about the world. It's … wonderful, really. Not the same as nice, or even good, but it's full of … stuff. We need never get to the end of it. There's always new stuff. *[Snapping out of it]* Yeah. All right. What shall we do now?

Johnny, Wobbler, Bigmac, and Yo-less exit.

THE END

Activities

JOHNNY AND THE DEAD ACTIVITIES

Key Stage 3 Framework Objectives	Relevant Activities Chapter(s)
Sentence Level	
13 b) recount	Battle in the Cemetery
13 d) instructions	Mastering New Technology
13 e) persuasion	Mastering New Technology
15 Vary formality	Mastering New Technology
Word Level	
12 Using a dictionary	What's in a Name?
14 Word meaning in context	What's in a Name?; Mastering New Technology
21 Subject vocabulary	Mastering New Technology
Reading	
1 Locate information	What's in a Name?; Battle in the Cemetery
2 Extract information	Tommy Atkins, The British Tommy; A New Scene; Battle in the Cemetery
4 Note-making	Tommy Atkins, The British Tommy
6 Active reading	Tommy Atkins, The British Tommy; A New Scene
7 Identify main ideas	Battle in the Cemetery
8 Infer and deduce	What's in a Name?; A New Scene
12 Character, setting and mood	What's in a Name?; Tommy Atkins, The British Tommy
14 Language choices	A New Scene; Battle in the Cemetery
Writing	
1 Drafting process	Mastering New Technology
2 Planning formats	The Development Debate
3 Exploratory writing	What's in a Name?
6 Characterisation	A New Scene
9 Link writing and reading	What's in a Name?; A New Scene
10 Organise texts appropriately	Battle in the Cemetery; Mastering New Technology
11 Present information	Mastering New Technology
13 Instructions and directions	Mastering New Technology
14 Evocative description	Battle in the Cemetery
15 Express a view	Mastering New Technology
Speaking and Listening	
1 Clarify through talk	Tommy Atkins, The British Tommy; A New Scene; The Development Debate; On the Stage
2 Recount	Battle in the Cemetery
3 Shape a presentation	Battle in the Cemetery
4 Answers, instructions, explanations	Mastering New Technology
5 Put a point of view	The Development Debate
6 Recall main points	Tommy Atkins, The British Tommy; The Development Debate

Key Stage 3 Framework Objectives	Relevant Activities Chapter(s)
7 Pertinent questions	Tommy Atkins, The British Tommy; Battle in the Cemetery; The Development Debate
10 Report main points	A New Scene
11 Range of roles	The Development Debate
12 Exploratory talk	On the Stage
13 Collaboration	On the Stage
14 Modify views	A New Scene; The Development Debate; On the Stage
15 Explore in role	Tommy Atkins, The British Tommy; Battle in the Cemetery; On the Stage
16 Collaborate on scripts	Tommy Atkins, The British Tommy; A New Scene; The Development Debate
17 Extend spoken repertoire	A New Scene; Battle in the Cemetery; The Development Debate
18 Exploratory drama	A New Scene
19 Evaluate presentations	Tommy Atkins, The British Tommy; On the Stage

JOHNNY AND THE DEAD ACTIVITIES

Key Stage 3 Framework Objectives	Relevant Activities Chapter(s)
Sentence Level	
9 Adapting text types	Mastering New Technology
12 Degrees of formality	Battle in the Cemetery; Mastering New Technology
Word Level	
7 c) words in context	What's in a Name?; Mastering New Technology
9 Specialist vocabulary	Mastering New Technology
Reading	
2 Independent research	Tommy Atkins, The British Tommy
3 Writing to reflect	Tommy Atkins, The British Tommy
4 Versatile reading	What's in a Name?
5 Trace developments	What's in a Name?; Tommy Atkins, The British Tommy
7 Implied and explicit meanings	What's in a Name?
8 Transposition	A New Scene
Writing	
2 Anticipate reader reaction	Mastering New Technology
3 Notemaking formats	The Development Debate
5 Narrative commentary	Battle in the Cemetery
6 Figurative language	Battle in the Cemetery
7 Establish the tone	What's in a Name?; A New Scene
10 Effective information	Mastering New Technology
12 Formal description	Mastering New Technology
13 Present a case persuasively	Mastering New Technology
Speaking and Listening	
2 Develop recount	Battle in the Cemetery
3 Formal presentation	The Development Debate
5 Questions to clarify or refine	Tommy Atkins, The British Tommy; Battle in the Cemetery; The Development Debate; Mastering New Technology
6 Evaluate own listening	A New Scene
7 Listen for a specific purpose	Tommy Atkins, The British Tommy; Battle in the Cemetery; The Development Debate; Mastering New Technology
10 Hypothesis and speculation	The Development Debate; On the Stage
11 Building on others	A New Scene; The Development Debate; On the Stage
12 Varied roles in discussion	What's in a Name?; Tommy Atkins, The British Tommy; The Development Debate
13 Evaluate own drama skills	On the Stage
14 Dramatic techniques	A New Scene; On the Stage
15 Work in role	Tommy Atkins, The British Tommy; A New Scene; Battle in the Cemetery; The Development Debate
16 Collaborative presentation	Tommy Atkins, The British Tommy; A New Scene; Mastering New Technology; The Development Debate; On the Stage

What's in a Name?

In Terry Pratchett's novels, the names of his characters are important. They often give clues as to the personality and interests of the characters.

DEAD FRIENDS

1 The names of the Dead have been carefully chosen by the author. How do they reflect the interests and lives of the Dead?

2 Skim the playscript to find references to these characters, then complete the grid below.

Name of character	Character's life	Link
Mrs Sylvia Liberty	A suffragette who campaigned to give the vote and more rights to women	
Solomon Einstein		
Addison Vincent Fletcher		
William Stickers		A 'sticker' is someone who is determined and will work hard for a purpose
Eric Grimm		

LIVING FRIENDS

1 Johnny has three close friends: Wobbler, Bigmac, and Yo-less. These names are nicknames. What do you think they suggest about the characters? Note down your initial thoughts.

2　Much of Pratchett's humour comes from people acting in an unexpected way, challenging our assumptions about them. For example, we are told in the novel that Bigmac 'had 'Blackbury Skins' on his T-shirt, a suede haircut, great big boots, great big braces and LOVE and HAT (the 'E' kept rubbing off) in Biro on his knuckles'. Bigmac has a tough image, but is he really tough?

When you have read the playscript, think about whether these characters acted in the way that you expected?

3　Skim the playscript to find evidence about the characters, and complete the grid below.

Nickname	What the nickname suggests	Actual character
Wobbler	Unsteady or clumsy; timid; tubby	
Bigmac		
Yo-less		West Indian; likes brass bands and doing extra homework

4　Pratchett shows how foolish it is to stereotype people (i.e. assume they have certain characteristics, just because of the way they look, their job, or their parents). There are several places where stereotypes are challenged. Find them in the text (looking in particular at Scenes 2, 7, and 15).

5　Think about the way that the Dead are portrayed. Does the author stick to stereotypes? The Dead dislike being referred to as 'ghosts'? Why do you think this is?

• •

UNITED AMALGAMATED CONSOLIDATED HOLDINGS

In pairs, discuss the name of the company 'United Amalgamated Consolidated Holdings'.

a) What do these words actually mean? (You may need to look them up in a dictionary.)

b) What impression do they convey of the company? Do they suggest
- power
- flexibility
- authority
- familiarity
- fairness
- openness?

c) Skim the playscript to find evidence of what the company is like.

d) Do you think the name is appropriate? Can you think of alternatives?

e) Share your ideas with the rest of the class.

Tommy Atkins, The British Tommy

Johnny wants to talk to Tommy Atkins, to find out about The Blackbury Pals Battalion, but he is too late. Tommy Atkins dies before Johnny can see him.

Imagine Johnny spots the name 'Mr T. Atkins' a few days earlier at the nursing home, and manages to meet him. Improvise the scene in pairs. First, think carefully about the two characters, how you might portray them, and what they might discuss:

- Skim the playscript for information about Tommy Atkins, and make brief notes. (Look at Scenes 5, 8, and 10.)

- Think about what objects Tommy might show Johnny.

- What sort of questions might Johnny ask? (For example, he might ask Tommy why he said 'I'm the one' when he showed Johnny his old army pay book.)

- Think about how Tommy might feel, remembering the First World War. His emotions might be mixed.

- If possible, do some more research about the Pals Battalions and add this information to what Tommy tells Johnny. (One of the most famous Battalions was The Accrington Pals, from East Lancashire. Many of the Pals were killed at the Battle of the Somme in July 1916.)

- Improvise the scene in front of the class.

- After the performance, the class could ask the 'characters' some questions. Remember to stay in role when answering: Tommy is 96, and may be a bit deaf and inclined to lose himself in his memories; Johnny may be struck by the fact that the young men who joined up, were not much older than himself and his friends (many boys lied about their age).

A New Scene

1   Read the extract from the novel, below.

It was very, very chilly inside the phone box.

'I must say, electricity is very easy to master when you're dead.'

'What are you doing, Mr Fletcher?'

'Very easy indeed. Who shall we talk to next?'

'We must speak to the Town Hall!'

'But it is a Saturday, Mrs Liberty. There will be no-one there.'

'Then try to find young Johnny. I don't know what he means about trying to find famous people buried in the cemetery. WE'RE here, after all.'

'I'll keep trying. It's amazingly easy to understand.'

'Where's Mr Stickers gone?'

'He's trying to listen to Radio Moscow, whatever that is. On the wireless telegraphy apparatus.'

'I say, this is rather invigorating, you know. I've never been out of the cemetery before.'

'Yes, it's a new lease of life.'

'You can escape from almost anything,' said Mr Vicenti.

There was a faint cough. They looked around.

Mr Grimm was watching them through the railings.

The dead seemed to sober up. They always became more serious in front of Mr Grimm.

They shuffled their spectral feet.

'You're outside,' said Mr Grimm. 'You know that's wrong.'

'Only a little way, Eric,' said the Alderman. 'That can't do any harm. It's for the good of the—'

'It's WRONG.'

'We don't have to listen to him,' said Mr Vicenti.

'You'll get into terrible trouble,' said Mr Grimm.

'No we won't,' said Mr Vicenti.

'It's dabbling with the Known,' said Mr Grimm. 'You'll get into dreadful trouble and it won't be my fault. You are bad people.'

He turned, and walked back to his grave.

'Dial the number,' said Mr Vicenti. The others seemed to wake up.

'You know,' said Mrs Liberty, 'he may have a point—'

'Forget about Mr Grimm,' said Mr Vicenti. He opened his hands. A white dove shot out of his sleeve and perched on the phone box, blinking.

2   In groups (of at least five), discuss where this scene might fit into the playscript.

3   Use the extract to write a new scene. Think carefully about:
- what to include and what to omit
- which character says what
- stage directions
- how to relay information from the narrative through actions, as well as speech (e.g. the temperature in the phone box).

4   When your scene is written, rehearse a performance. Discuss and decide:
- what your characters look like, their body language and facial expressions
- the tone in which they speak, and where this might change as their mood alters
- where pauses might be effective
- how to give the impression of the dove appearing from Mr Vicenti's sleeve.

5   Stage a performance in front of the class. Ask the class for comments, e.g. which parts worked well, and invite suggestions for improvement.

Battle in the Cemetery

DIARY ENTRY

1   Re-read the beginning of Scene 15 (up until Johnny's living friends leave him on page 69).

2   Imagine you are Johnny, or one of his friends, writing in his diary later that evening. Write a recount the events. Remember that a recount:
    - uses the past tense
    - has a clear time sequence
    - uses connecting words, such as 'first', 'then', 'after', 'later', 'finally'.

Your chosen character may not see all the action in the cemetery; for example, both Wobbler and Bigmac go off to find help. You may need to describe what happens 'offstage'. In your diary entry, you might want to include personal feelings, as well as a description of the events.

AT THE POLICE STATION

1   In the playscript, the police take the thugs 'for a nice little ride down to Blackbury nick'. Imagine that they take the boys, too, to give a verbal recount of what happened that evening.

    Think about how you would recount the events to the police. Remember:
    - the details are important, such as exact times and places
    - your descriptions of the people and events need to be accurate
    - the police need to know the facts rather than your opinions and feelings
    - to keep in the role of your chosen character.

Cut 2 lines ?

2   Recount the events to the police (i.e. your class). The class should listen carefully to the recount, then ask questions to clarify anything that is not clear or that has been left out.

The Development Debate

In the 1980s, Westminster Council sold three cemeteries in North London for fifteen pence, in order to save the cost of maintaining the grounds. The company that bought the cemeteries then sold them on, for £2.5 million! There was a public outcry and many questions were asked: should be land have been sold at all? Should the dead be left to rest? Why was the land sold so cheaply in the first place? Public inquiries and reports followed, costing the Council, and therefore the taxpayer, millions of pounds.

The development of sites for buildings, roads, parks, etc. often causes fierce debate as people have strong feeling and important interests. Hold a debate in your class.

PREPARATION

1 Choose a real or fictional development, e.g. the building of a new road/immigration centre/theme park/shopping centre/football stadium near where you live.

2 Decide whether you are 'for' or 'against' the development (or you may wish to stay 'floating' and decide whether you are 'for' or 'against' during the debate).

3 Take on the role of a person with a specific interest in the development, e.g. the manager of the building firm; an elderly man whose house will have to be demolished; a campaigner for the preservation of rare plants or birds; a local parent; someone who works at the local tourist information office; a council representative; a local shopkeeper; the local headteacher, etc.

4 Appoint someone to chair the debate and speakers to represent a) those for the development, and b) those against the development.

5 In the two groups, prepare your arguments as to why you think the development should/should not go ahead. Think

about jobs, noise, congestion, transport, and the environment. Make notes and then organize them into a logical sequence.

6 Guess what the other group might say, and think about how you could argue against them.

● ●

THE DEBATE

The format of the debate should be as follows:
- The chairperson opens the debate with a brief outline of what is proposed.
- The spokesperson for one group speaks.
- The spokesperson for the other group speaks.
- The debate is open to all other people.
- The chairperson briefly sums up the arguments on each side.
- Everyone votes on whether the development goes ahead or not.

Remember to stay in role, throughout the debate. Each person who speaks should introduce himself or herself, and explain who they are (i.e. their role).

Mastering New Technology

WRITING INSTRUCTIONS

Addison Fletcher and Solomon Einstein put together their scientific and practical skills in order to make things work for them, such as the old television set and the telephone. If they weren't among the Dead, Johnny would have to explain things more clearly to the others.

1   Imagine you are Johnny, explaining to Alderman Thomas Bowler and Mrs Sylvia Liberty how to send a text message, or how to write a letter/play a game on a computer.

  ● Draw a simple sketch of the equipment, labelling the important parts. You may need more than one sketch.
  ● Give instructions in a clear sequence, possibly using numbers to explain the process, step-by-step.
  ● Use the imperative form of the verb, e.g. 'Press the button .../Switch on the ...'
  ● Be precise in your instructions, giving clear detail.
  ● Keep the instructions short and simple.
  ● Try not to use words that may confuse the Dead (for instance, they will not know what a computer 'mouse' is!).
  ● Add a short section at the end called 'Troubleshooting'. In this section, explain what to do if the user makes mistakes. Alternatively, add a short section entitled 'Do not ...' and list things to avoid.

2   In pairs, swap instructions. Take on the role of either Alderman Thomas Bowler or Mrs Sylvia Liberty, as you read the instructions. Do they make sense? If not, ask your partner questions. You may need to redraft your written instructions in the light of these questions.

WRITING ADVERTS

1   In pairs, write a short radio advert for a technical product, e.g. a mobile phone that can send text messages. Imagine you are trying to sell your product to older people, who may not have sent text messages before. You will need to explain, very simply, how the product works, and why they should buy it. Think about:

- persuasive language
- repetition to emphasize your product
- a memorable 'jingle' or 'slogan'
- clear reasons why your product is the best on the market
- how much technical detail you need to explain (too much may put people off).

ACTIVITIES

JOHNNY AND THE DEAD

On the Stage

THE STAGE

Johnny and the Dead has been adapted in such a way that the play can be performed in a classroom without many props or complex scenery. However, think carefully about how you could stage the action. Discuss the advantages and disadvantages of each of the following methods:

- **In the round,** with the audience surrounding the central 'stage' area

- **End on,** with the audience just at the front of the stage

- **Promenade,** with both the audience and the actors free to move about the room as they wish, with no designated 'stage' area.

Think about:

- how many actors appear at one time

- whether you want characters to make specific entrances and exits, or whether it might be more effective for them to drift on and off stage informally.

SCENE CHANGES AND PROPS

Discuss how you could convey the following scenes using simple, classroom props:
- the cemetery
- the classroom
- Grandad's house
- the library
- the shopping mall
- Sunshine Acres
- the chapel
- the canal
- the civic centre.

Remember that the props need to be easy for the actors to move as they come on and off stage. You will not want to break the pace of the play with long scene changes.

● ●

PORTRAYING THE DEAD

1   Wobbler (unable to see the Dead himself) asks Johnny whether the Dead are 'lurching'. He remembers the traditional portrayal of the Dead as clumsy, threatening, and dangerous. Johnny doesn't see the Dead like this. He sees them as individuals, like the living. But how could you distinguish the Dead from the 'living' on a stage? Consider:

- the use of dry ice or smoke pellets
- make-up and costumes
- lighting
- music
- the reaction of the other actors onstage (e.g. Johnny's friends cannot see the Dead but feel uneasy in their presence)
- how the Dead might move slightly differently from the living
- how you could convey the difficulties that the Dead have with handling objects, e.g. the newspaper.

2   After discussing the staging, the props, and the portrayal of the Dead, organize a performance of one scene to test your ideas. Review your work, and reflect on possible improvements.

Further Activities

1   'There's a world out there, and we helped to make it...'
    says Alderman Bowler in Scene 11. Find out more about
    one of the following:
    a) the suffragettes
    b) Karl Marx
    c) Albert Einstein
    d) Alexander Graham Bell.

Use the Internet as well as other sources to gather information
about your chosen subject. What contribution did he or she
make to our society?

2   Read some poems written during WW1 (e.g. by Siegfried
    Sassoon, Wilfred Owen, Robert Graves, or Rupert
    Brooke). What do you learn about life in the trenches?

3 The Imperial War Museum in London has a collection of old posters from WW1. Many posters were printed by the government and are persuasive texts, encouraging people to join up and participate in the war effort. Look at the posters and discuss how effective you think they might have been.

4 Johnny and his friends try to think of ways of describing the Dead in a 'politically correct' and inoffensive way. For example, they refer to the Dead as 'post-senior citizens', 'breathily challenged', and 'vertically disadvantaged'. Discuss the value of political correctness and when it becomes extreme. Think up some 'politically correct' terms of your own.